The Hijacker

Overcome
Self-Sabotaging
Behavior

By Lauren Doyle

The Hijacker
Overcome Self-Sabotaging Behavior

Published by Getting Results
1290 N Palm Ave.
Sarasota, FL 34236

ISBN: 978-1974174843

DISCLAIMER AND/OR LEGAL NOTICES

While the publisher and authors have used their best efforts in preparing this book, they make no representations or warranties with respect to the accuracy or completeness of the contents of this book. The advice and strategies contained herein may not be suitable for your situation. You should consult a professional where appropriate. Neither the publisher nor the authors shall be liable for any loss of profit or any other commercial damages, including but not limited to special, incidental, consequential, or other damages. The purchaser or reader of this publication assumes responsibility for the use of these materials and information. Adherence to all applicable laws and regulations, both advertising and all other aspects of doing business in the United States or any other jurisdiction, is the sole responsibility of the purchaser or reader.

This book is intended to provide accurate information with regards to the subject matter covered. However, the Author and the Publisher accept no responsibility for inaccuracies or omissions, and

This book is dedicated to the all of the clients I've had the privilege of working with over the years. Little do they know that I learn just as much from them as they do from me. It brings great joy to celebrate their successes with them each week.

Table of Contents

Introduction

I've written this book to inspire you to take action to overcome self-sabotaging behavior, which is a challenge all of us face at one time or another. As a business coach, one of the hardest tasks I have is to help others "get out of their own way" and follow through on the actions they recognize (or come to recognize) they need to do in order to fulfill their long-desired goals.

It is important to note why I wrote this book. After coaching individuals for nearly 20 years, I heard the following statement too many times to ignore: "Your firm (Getting Results, Inc.) is not the first coaching company I've tried…." Naturally, I wanted to inquire why there were so many "program hoppers" as I call them. They jump from program to program not feeling like they were that effective for them. Now, I know a lot of these programs and I know they deliver great content, so my inquiry went deeper. Why were these professionals – clearly driven professionals – not getting the results they desired in other programs. What made us different? This was the critical question. Our coaches don't have the magic pill – but what we do have is a deep understanding of two things: 1) Helping others gain clarity on a design that fits "who" they are and their personality well, and 2) How to help others "get out of their own way." In other words, help them overcome self-sabotaging behavior.

Getting to the core of both of these two key elements of our success required a deeper understanding of the topic I cover in this book. As you will read, a hijacker currently has control of your mind. How can you possibly master your own destiny (or direction of your life and business) if you are completely unaware that you are not even in the driver's seat? My goal in writing this book is to help you unseat the hijacker that is currently in charge so that you can retake control of the outcomes in your life and your business.

Just a note on how to read this book: This is not just an informational book about what Human Operating Systems are but also a guide. The first half provides an explanation and understanding of what Human Operating Systems are. The second half of the book walks you through a number of steps to identify your own operating system and help you take back control from your hijacker.

In the book, I've also outlined a number of Human Operating Systems that I've recognized to date. You may be one who finds reading about each HOS to be fascinating, or you may find that you lose interest in reading about operating systems that you don't feel fit you well. Either way, I encourage you to continue to read through the end of the book. Knowing about the HOS of others will be extremely helpful with your interactions with them. If you feel the need to skip ahead and revisit the individual descriptions of the operating systems later, that is fine, too.

Please know that this book is meant to be an interactive guide. Once you get to an exercise I describe, be sure to follow through on the exercise – don't just read past it. My goal is to coach you though this book to help you understand your own operating system and learn to effectively manage it, so you can create your life as you intend. This is called a Life (or Business) by Design. The only way to do this effectively is to unseat the hijacker, as it is the primary source of consternation you experience in life.

Keep in mind that your hijacker is a very close "friend." He's been with you the majority of your life, so it can be difficult to recognize at first, especially if you don't have someone you can speak to that is an objective party. If you need additional resources to help you understand your HOS, please visit www.TheHijacker.net.

Introduction

I Unseated the Hijacker in My Life

It was a beautiful afternoon in sunny San Diego. I pulled up in front of my house in my new red convertible, top down. I was compelled to stop at the top of the hill as the ocean view took my breath away. It was the kind of picture that forces you to stop, take a moment, and reflect on life. I was suddenly overwhelmed with a feeling of gratefulness for having the opportunity to have created this amazing life for myself at the young age of 21. It was also a very defining moment.

While I knew that most 21-year-olds would have died for the opportunity that I currently had – six-figure income, red convertible, fabulous home with a killer view – I also realized that the number of hours I was working to make this possible was negating my ability to really live life fully. Yes, I had moments of enjoying the literal and figurative view, but they were only that – moments. I'd moved to San Diego just after graduating with my bachelor's degree to establish residency as I applied to just one graduate program at San Diego State University.

I was suddenly struck by what I might miss out on if I continued working the tremendous number of hours I was. I would effectively miss out on life, only enjoying "moments" of it at a time. I was living by default. However, it was hard to say "no" to the families that needed me, the ones who sung my praises to other parents who were also in great need of an experienced therapist to work with their autistic children. I was working six days a week from 7:00 a.m. until 9:00 p.m. most days.

So I began to devise a plan: a plan that allowed me to make decent money, help families, and still have a life of my own to enjoy.

This was my first insight into what it meant to truly design a life or lifestyle. At that moment, at the top of the hill with a beautiful vista in front of me, I'm not sure I knew what it meant to have a life by design rather than default, but it turned out to be one of the most useful epiphanies of my life, but it certainly was not the last.

No one would argue that I was a driven person. I strived to be the best and to end up on top. While this sounds great, it isn't without its shortcomings. I charged forward to attack whatever it was I wanted. I did so with so-called blinders on. Let me explain.

You see, when something didn't go exactly my way, I dropped it... without a second thought. This applied to interests, hobbies, opportunities and even my relationships.

I had a tendency to have an "it's my way or the highway" mentality when it came to relationships. As a result, I dated *a lot* and I also ended *a lot* of relationships. I missed out on the rewards of long-term, meaningful relationships because the second they didn't fit my needs, I quit.

I quit hobbies or sports that I was not immediately good at.

I pursued opportunities for the challenge and to conquer them. I even nearly gave up the career opportunity of a lifetime to pursue a doctorate degree in a different city and nearly gave up the amazing life and relationships I had created for that pursuit.

Without even knowing it, I was living a life by default – guided by the hijacker who had inadvertently taken over the driver's seat of my life. It's like he had me blindfolded, holding a "fake" steering wheel to make me believe I was in control. It was just a short time later that I would discover the surprise. My eyes would be opened to a whole new reality; a reality where I regained conscious control of my life. I say it was a surprise because I didn't think there was anything "wrong." I was "fine." At least, I thought I was fine. After all, how much did I really know at the age of 22? Had I continued this pattern, I may have found myself old, frustrated, and still jumping from one relationship to another had I not unseated my hijacker.

There were patterns… there always are. However, for the most part, it takes time – a lot of time – to discover patterns, how they show up, and how they affect our lives. At 22, I was too young to fully understand the patterns that were developing in my life, but I had glimpses – and lucky for me, I had chosen a career that forced you to uncover and dissect patterns in human behavior.

The Blessing is the Curse

There was no doubt I got whatever it was I wanted (or at least what I thought I wanted). This was my blessing – and my curse.

I would drive to achieve and accomplish for the sheer sake of achieving and accomplishing, often failing to see how it fit into the bigger picture… ah, the big picture. We will talk more about how we can become blinded to the big picture by focusing on the small and now.

I feel lucky to have had parents who rarely said "no," who encouraged me to do whatever it was I wanted because they believed I could accomplish it. It might have been their belief that later became my own belief that I could accomplish whatever I wanted to. Or perhaps it was pure selfishness of wanting it all and being just naïve enough to believe I could have it or create it. As I sat in my car that day looking over the ocean, I knew I still had the drive to accomplish, but I wanted to do it my way – without giving up everything or without failing to have the time to enjoy it.

This began the journey to figure out what exactly it meant to live a life by design; to live a life that was not hyper-focused on the small, immediate objectives and accomplishments, but a life that achieved the overall, grand vision – the big picture.

Figuring It Out

We're all blessed with certain gifts and talents, and mine happens to be the ability and desire to figure things out… how things work and how to fix them when they don't. This was the talent I employed to create the life I now live by design. When I had my epiphany at the top of the hill overlooking the ocean, I didn't know how to change this, but I knew I had the desire to figure it out. That learning process brought me to understand that everyone has a hijacker that causes them to self-sabotage their lives, and through the process, I learned how to unseat mine.

I failed at trying to conform to doing things the way most people my age were. I hated having a boss and liked making my own hours. I liked and wanted to do things "my way." Doing things traditionally didn't suit me at all. In fact, my first marriage ended after a year and a half because he wanted a very traditional marriage in which he envisioned that the wife would stay home and didn't have any unmarried friends and the husband would be the sole breadwinner and household leader. He was a great guy; however, we had two very different ideas of our relationship "designs," and I wasn't going to compromise mine.

After that marriage ended (I can't say "failed" because it was what it was, and it was also part of my learning process to unseat my hijacker), I sat down with pen, paper, and a bottle of wine and began writing a list of everything I wanted in a significant other, a partner. The more wine I drank, the more detailed I got with my desires. When all of my ideas ran dry and I couldn't think of any additional characteristics, I sat back and reviewed my list: Intelligent. Respectful of the carefree lifestyle I enjoyed and had designed for myself and who would honor that, understanding that it wasn't a hippie or lazy thing. Someone who wanted to play a lot, travel, was active and enjoyed being outdoors. I wanted an adventurer with whom I could experience life. I wanted someone with blue eyes and dark skin "who tanned well" (and at this point, it might have been the wine talking). I wanted someone who was committed to his own development, who thrived on learning as much as I did and who wouldn't settle for boring. Yes, the list went on and on and on, but I was working on figuring out a relationship by design that blended with my life by design.

Here's the funny part: About three years after meeting my eventual spouse and upon moving to Charleston, SC, we were unpacking boxes. I found my now husband, Ken, engrossed in a piece of paper with a smirk on his face. When he looked up, I asked, "What are you reading?" He tossed the paper to me. I started to laugh as soon as I saw it. It was The List. The list I hadn't seen for about four years. The list I'd created over a bottle of wine envisioning everything I had ever wanted in a guy. Crazy enough, I was unpacking with the man who encompassed 41 of the 42 traits I'd listed. Fortunately, the one trait on which I compromised was "tan well." Ken is Irish and turns pink, not brown. "I can live with this," I thought, and the next year, we married on the beach of Isle of Palms.

The Next Puzzle Box

I had been getting better and better at figuring out how to put puzzles together – the puzzles that surround the "how do I accomplish this?" sort of thinking… the puzzles that are inherent in figuring out how to do things by design rather than allowing them to happen around us by default. I was always figuring out how to live proactively rather than reactively. Within a reasonably short period of time, I could complete the picture for each design, and I was creating a formula for the process. It was never a question of "if," but rather only "how" I could do something.

As Ken and I talked about what we really wanted, escaping winter was the recurring idea. We realized we wanted to be snowbirds. Lakehouse in Michigan, winters in the south. This is obviously not a common approach: snowbirds at age 30. When you think of snowbirds, it depicts an image of gray-haired 70-somethings who have worked hard all their lives, raised their kids, put them through college, and now… finally… after all these years can live their own lives and have fun. Maybe it was because I was never told that something could be impossible, I decided that I didn't want until my hips needed to be replaced to have fun and enjoy life without cold weather. This presented a puzzle to figure out that would ultimately lead me to designing a life and a business that would support the mobility to escape winter every year.

Like many couples, there were ideas and opportunities that arose for us. It was tempting to jump on many of them. We entertained the thought of several business opportunities, but the barometer of whether or not something was a fit for our lifestyle always boiled down to understanding and clarifying our design commitments. Would we still be able to live in multiple places? Would we still be able to spend our afternoons greeting our daughter when she came home from pre-school?

A huge piece and, in fact, the very foundation of the ability to create and live into our design, be it a business design, relationship design or overall lifestyle design, is to understand and recognize the hijacker we each have in our lives. Had we been asleep and at the whims of our respective hijackers, our decisions would not have led us in the direction that supported the ultimate design we created for our lives. By default, Ken would still be working in corporate America, tied to an office in a big city, and I might still be in school, earning yet another unnecessary degree. Instead, we're living the lives that we want to now… not at age 70 and not according to what anyone else thinks is right.

The Lessons

I've shared my story because the epiphany I had and the process I went through to understand and create my own life by design is integral to helping you to do the same. I hope that by knowing my story, you have better insight into the difference of living by design rather than default. I've found some people hear the words without truly being able to differentiate the concepts. Or they don't realize the triggers that derail design and revert to default. Most of us, like myself, tried to "piecemeal" a life together – looking at various aspects of life as separate from one another – achieving career accomplishments in one bucket, searching for a relationship in another bucket, neighborhood/city home life in a separate bucket. We often create "buckets" that may not fit together which leaves a life of frustration, discontentedness, or is simply lackluster.

I learned a lot along the way, and here are a couple of things that I learned and know to be entirely true. First, most people, if not everyone, would say that they want to have a life, business, and relationship by design. Yes, they say they want their ideal outcome; however, few believe it's possible to achieve because of default programming. Default programming comes from parents, teachers, friends, and communities. Default programming comes from our own hardwiring. Default programing comes from our internal operating systems – that which I call your Human Operating System or HOS.

You most likely know someone who seems to have an ideal design (as least from what may be apparent to you), but most people are still trying to define their design or are too caught up in "getting through life" that they don't believe they have the time or mental space to create the design. Perhaps you fall into this category. If so, congratulations. You have a lot of company, and, more importantly, you're about to learn how to changes things. You're about to learn who your hijacker is and how to stop him from sabotaging your life.

The greatest obstacle to achieving your design is your unconsciousness to your own HOS. That's about to change. Why? First, you can't manage something that you don't know even exists in the first place. Only with awareness can you begin to bring about change... change that is the result of managing your hijacker. That said, I'll warn you: While the concept is understandable (and your recognition might be immediate as you read through the chapters that define each HOS type) and even when you know about it, managing it can still be very uncomfortable. You've been so accustomed to the way things have been, that changing things – even when working to change them for the better and to change them to align with and support your design and desired outcome – can be scary. The majority of people don't like change. The known road, even if represents being a rut, is a very comfortable one.

Finally, I know that most people believe that the solutions are outside of them. These are the people who are living by default and reacting to events and whatever happens in their lives. They might be very talented and have a large toolbox of skills that enable them to react with

15

some success; however, they're still reacting. When you're reacting, you're not controlling the outcome, and no matter how successful you might be at reacting, you're also wasting time. In essence, every time you react, you've wasted some of your life that could be spent doing what you want, spent on implementing your design. Every time you react, you're self-sabotaging the very things you desire.

So let's get started!

Chapter One:
Unlock Your Operating System

Patterns exist everywhere, and consider the definition of a pattern: a form or model, a natural or chance configuration, or a reliable sample of traits, acts, tendencies or other observable characteristics of a person. Ah, that last one, the one about traits, acts, and tendencies, that's the one. And the word "reliable" plays an important part in that definition. The very nature of a pattern is reliable repetition… a thing to be repeated over and over.

We all exhibit patterns, and patterns in a person's life are very telling… that is if you know how to decode them. Most people don't. In fact, most people can't even decode their own patterns, no matter how many times they're repeated.

Each one of us has our own reality – not shared with anyone else. You have one perception – your own. One viewpoint – your own. Try asking someone who has never lived outside of Idaho to explain what it's like to live in the Caribbean, in Mexico, or in New York City. They can't because they have never lived an alternate reality, an alternate life. Patterns make people. Patterns create lives.

I've written this book because I understand that patterns are revealing, but the most important thing about them – in fact, the only way to really design and live the life you want – is to be able to decode them. Decoding those patterns helps us understand what purpose they serve. They reveal what blind spots we have. These blind spots are harmful if not uncovered. They cause the greatest frustrations and heartache in our lives. In my line of work and in coaching through the years, I've heard so many people say things at the start of our work together like, "I've been to many counselors and none has helped." Or "I worked with a coach and what they suggested worked… for a while, but then things got mucky again, and the same problems cropped up."

The latter statement doesn't really surprise me because the previous counselor/coach/therapist failed to decode the pattern. I'm happy to tell you that one of the other statements we've heard in our business is, "You weren't the first coach I went to but you were the last." Why? Because of the results. Not because I have some sort of magic fairy dust, but because I've been able to uncover the diagnostic code and that makes all the difference. Without understanding the diagnostic code, you will never arrive at a solution.

Imagine you had an issue with your car, and that issue occurred over and over and over. So you took it to your mechanic who systematically repaired and replaced various parts only to have the issue recur. Frustrating, right? Why can't he just fix it for good? The problem is that the mechanic is not truly identifying what's wrong. He's looking at the symptoms and patterns of the problem, but until he gets to the real underlying issue, he'll keep trying to replace parts in an attempt to solve the problem.

That analogy has a certain 20th century ring to it because now mechanics can run the diagnostics on the car's built-in software to get the diagnostic code that will lead them to the solution. Ah, the diagnostic code. That code leads to the accurate solution and repair of the problem.

This is a similar challenge people have when they repeatedly try various therapists, counselors, coaches, and consultants. If those professionals are not able to accurately uncover the diagnostic code, they'll be fairly ineffective at achieving the desired end result. This isn't to say that there wouldn't be certain improvements; there most certainly would be, even if only for a short time as long as the client or participant was actively following through on the "program." However, without the diagnostic code, you'll never get the solution you need to achieve what you want. Without the diagnostic code, you're bound to continue self-sabotaging your own results.

You find yourself going through the same struggle over and over and facing the same challenge or challenges repeatedly. And to be blunt, you will continue to do that until you understand your own diagnostic code. Perhaps you face the same problem repeatedly in your marriage or relationship but can never seem to finally get past it… for good. Or you're working like crazy and dedicating your entire life to your business but can never break through to the level you want.

The good news is that we all actually have a diagnostic code. This code is what I refer to as the Human Operating System. It's operating behind the scenes and driving most of your behavior. If you're one who's been to various counselors or therapists without getting a permanent way to overcome the repeated patterns and behaviors that stand in your way, it's highly likely that (even for the most well-trained, highly counseled or coached individuals) you have not accurately had your operating system diagnosed. As a result, you continuously try to fix, repair, and resolve the issues and challenges that seem to continue to creep back into your life over and over again. Just like that mechanic who keeps replacing and repairing parts without ever actually fixing the car for good.

The only way to effectively create your desired outcomes in business, your career, relationships, and in your life is to be able to practice Conscious Discernment. Conscious Discernment is having the ability to be fully aware of your choices and make the proper choice that is in alignment with your bigger commitments. When you are unware of your unconscious drivers, when you have too many blind spots, you don't have the ability to practice Conscious Discernment. You may think you have a clear design in your world, but I submit that that design is still a result of your unconscious driver – what I call the hijacker of your life. Unless you've had your Human Operating System identified and brought into the forefront of your consciousness, it's still running your life in the background.

The goal of this book is to help you figure out your diagnostic code… your Human Operating System. Until you fully understand that, you won't be able to live out the design you create for your business, relationships, or your life. However, while we all have a specific diagnostic code, learning what it is takes some work. It's not like we can hook your brain up to another computer, like your mechanic does with your car, and get the answer (well, not yet anyway). But I assure you, it's worth the effort, and I ask you to bear with me before we get to the heart of uncovering your Human Operating System as we fully explore the principle.

Brainwashing

Wouldn't it be crazy if you had the ability to brainwash your own brain... your own mind to have the opportunity to create the life of your dreams. Let me preface this by saying that this is not another book that uses magical motivation to change your life. This concept – brainwashing your own brain – requires you to complete the exercises of self-awareness to teach you how to manage your own mind. Yes, I did say "manage your own mind." Think about that one for a moment. Who exactly is doing the thinking if it is about your mind? Is your mind separate from the thinker or a part of it? Perhaps you never thought of your mind as something that could and should be managed. Without learning to manage your mind, you are destined to continue on the path of self-sabotage.

We all want things in life. I don't necessarily mean material things, but there are ideas or aspirations that we hope to one day realize. Some people dream bigger while others' dreams might be defined as "moderate." Some have grand goals while others are more simplistic. Regardless of the size or complexity of your aspirations, it behooves you to know all you can about how your own mind can help or hinder your goals.

The wild truth about achieving what you want does not necessarily come down to who beats the pavement harder, who tries harder, or who works harder. In some cases that may be true, but mostly your success in achievement can be a much straighter line if you understand how your mind operates at its core and how to manage and manipulate it. For most people, achieving success (that is, getting from where they are to where they want to be) is a circuitous route that doubles back on itself at times and takes some erratic turns. If mapped out, it looks far more like a squiggly, meandering line than a straight one. I'm certain you'll agree that a straight line is the quicker route to success.

Here's a simple example about the quicker route to success: take a master carpenter versus his apprentice. They may both get the job done eventually, but the master carpenter knows his tools better. He knows exactly where to go for the tool he needs to get the job done faster and more efficiently; whereas, the apprentice may spend a lot of time trying different tools to do the same job. He may need to test some different ways of getting the same job done. In the end, he may end up with the same completed project (maybe not with the same quality), but it would certainly take him a lot more time and with a greater amount of frustration than the master carpenter who strategized the job intimately knowing the tools he had to work with.

In this book, I hope to provide you with the knowledge you'll need to be more like the master carpenter and create a straighter line toward what you want to achieve. But knowledge is a tricky thing.

You see, there are a lot of things in this world that we know we know. For example, you may know that you know how to add (you know that 2+2=4) or you know that you know the number of miles you travel to get to the office. Then there are a lot of things you know that you don't know. For example, you may know that you don't know much about quantum physics or you may also be quite certain that you don't know how to speak Hungarian.

Those two things – knowing what we know and knowing what we don't know – are clear. But where things get interesting is once we start to consider the vast world of the things you don't even know you don't know. That's the tricky part of knowledge: not knowing what it is we do not know.

This part of your knowledge is so immense that you wouldn't even know where to discover all of the information that you don't know you don't know. Because of course, you don't realize that there is critical information about your success and functioning in this world, so you won't... even can't... know where to begin to look for that knowledge. In a nutshell, you can't ask a question to gain that knowledge because you don't know what to ask or that you even need to ask in the first place.

I can't impart everything that you don't know you don't know because there's still a world full of that information I'm trying to discover for myself. What I am going to share with you throughout this book, however, is a vital piece of your mental construct that has been dictating how your life turns out. We all like to believe that we are in the driver's seat of this thing called life. Let me throw you a curveball: Thinking you are in the driver's seat in the vehicle of your life is an illusion. You'll be shocked to know someone else is operating the steering wheel as well as the brake and the accelerator. Perhaps you have not been in control at all!

I'm here to tell you that some stranger has hijacked your ride. It is such a savvy hijacker, so well-trained, that you weren't even aware of when or how he took over piloting your life.

You know that you have experienced general frustrations in your life... but you just figure "that's life." Things happen. Everyone deals with these things at some point in their lives. But your frustrations are different. They seem to consistently appear. Patterns emerge. Ah, yes... the patterns. But just like a fish cannot comprehend an alternate reality other than living in water, you also cannot comprehend that there is any other way of understanding your place in the world. Perhaps you cannot comprehend your own self-sabotaging behavior and the fact that the only thing standing between you and what you want is, well, you. You're consistently getting in your own way.

Like I said, patterns in a person's life are very telling. Take Sam, for example. He was a miserably successful man. Of course, you're thinking miserably successful? Those words don't seem to go together. Let me explain: From the outside, men and women alike were very envious of him. He seemed to turn anything he touched into gold. He drove a new Ferrari every year, traveled to exotic places (when he had the time), and you guessed it, he lived in that house... you know the one: the mansion, the one everyone talked about. He oozed success from every pore; however, no matter how much money he made, how many employees he had, it was never enough. He wanted more. Wanting more is not necessarily a bad thing, but he wanted more at the expense of his marriages, relationships with friends, and maybe most importantly, his own peace of mind. The desire for more caused Sam to sabotage what he already had. So yes, he was miserably successful.

Now think about the guy who's financially successful, has an amazing marriage, fabulous kids, and loves what he does for a living. Have you ever considered what is different about that guy? May I submit that he has learned the ultimate game of mind management? It is my experience that people like "that guy" have committed themselves to a life of continual development – always working to improve themselves. Sam, on the other hand, has not. Sam's hijacker is clearly driving the vehicle of his life while the guy who can manage his mind is in control, steering where he wants, braking when needed, and accelerating as he chooses.

What I'm about share with you in this book will allow you to take back the wheel; it will allow you to get rid of your hijacker – the one you'll come to recognize as you read through the book. It will help you get out of your own way. I have shared this concept over the years with hundreds of individuals, and hands down, they have indicated that this has made the greatest impact on achieving the objectives they set out for themselves.

It's All about Your Operating System

I have to confess something, I hate writing. However, the fact that this book exists – the fact that you're holding it – is a testament to how strongly I believe that this concept (or theory, if you prefer) changes people's worlds. You see, I have been coaching individuals to create their ideal lives and businesses for nearly two decades. I have worked with people who have created great levels of success, but who are bored or otherwise unhappy. I've also worked with individuals who were just starting to figure out the paths for their lives. I've worked with couples to help them put their relationship back together so both people find it rewarding. In all cases, this work – managing their minds and decoding their patterns – has been an integral part of those clients getting the results they wanted to achieve…. of helping them to overcome self-sabotaging behavior.

I am so excited to share this concept with you because I have witnessed the impact it has on so many of the lives of people with whom I interact. I, too, have personally experienced the benefits of understanding my particular blind spot and how it literally carved a path for me that had both many benefits but also impeded many areas of my world. My goal at the end of this book is to have you become crystal clear as to who the hijacker of your life is and also how to manage that hijacker effectively and put yourself back in the driver's seat. The benefits you will reap are unlike any you can imagine. Once you're out of your own way, the path to success is far speedier.

What I am going to share with you is unlike any concept you have read about in the many books that came before this one. I am not disparaging any of them. There are hundreds of amazing and helpful books out there. Maybe you've read one or more of them, but up until this point, it was actually your hijacker reading those books to you, so you didn't get the full benefit of their messages.

Bear with me. Subjects like these can be tough to comprehend because we are trying to describe or understand something we cannot physically see. It's a lot like your computer. Actually, it's like your computer's operating system. You can see your computer and its components, and you can control the components – moving the mouse, keystroking entries – but what's producing the real results is the operating system. You may think it's a particular software program or app, but without a fully functioning operating system, it's all pretty useless.

Let me share information from *How Stuff Works*, "How Operating Systems Work" by Curt Franklin and Dave Coustan to paint a clearer picture:

"When you turn on your computer, it's nice to think that you're in control. There's the trusty computer mouse, which you can move anywhere on the screen, summoning up your music library or internet browser at the slightest whim. Although it's easy to feel like a director in front of your desktop or laptop, there's a lot going on inside, and the real man behind the curtain handling the necessary tasks is the operating system.

"Most desktop or laptop PCs come pre-loaded with Microsoft Windows. Macintosh computers come pre-loaded with Mac OS X. Many corporate servers use the Linux or UNIX operating systems. The operating system (OS) is the first thing loaded onto the computer – without the operating system, a computer is useless."

You have an operating system that is also working behind the scenes. And like your computer's operating system, you probably never think about it... until there's a crash, something that derails you on your journey.

Perhaps you know that your computer operating system needs an occasional tune up. If it hasn't been properly maintained or cleaned up over time, the system can become overwhelmed and start losing efficiency, becoming sluggish, and not functioning as it should. Remember Sam from earlier in the chapter? The guy who had it all but still wasn't happy? Sam definitely has an operating system that needs attention.

One of the other functions of your computer's operating system is to balance resources to keep things moving smoothly. If you're running a software program that demands a lot of memory, your computer's operating system will adjust behind the scenes, so your program runs as it should. The problem with the Human Operating System is that balancing resources is not its proficiency. In fact, the Human Operating System will almost always direct resources to accomplish one task: cover up insecurity.

Targeting Your Design

So what is it that you really want out of your life? Since you're reading this book, I'm pretty certain you've given this quite a bit of thought. You've probably also set goals to achieve what you want. I'll also wager that some, if not all, of your goals are directed to something tangible: earn more money, create my own business, earn a certain academic degree, etc. Those are certainly lofty and admirable targets. But they're the small targets, and when you get focused on the small target, you can't even see the big target – the one that you really want – greater balance and happiness in your life.

Here's the comparison I want you to keep in mind: Think about a sheet of paper and the wall of your office. The sheet of paper is certainly much smaller in size and scope. A standard sheet of paper is 8.5 by 11 inches. Your wall is likely 8 by 10 feet. The sheet of paper represents those tangible targets or goals I mentioned as the small ones – earn more, generate more sales, get that degree or certification, etc. It might be thought of as the day-to-day or short-term aspirations. I want to close this deal. I want to increase my sales by 30 percent. I want to buy a boat. Those targets are the sheet of paper.

Now think about the bigger target – the wall. That target is very likely similar for each one of us. We want to be happy, to have balance in our lives, and to live lives that matter and make a difference. The wall is so much larger than the sheet of paper that you'd imagine it's easier to hit the larger target. You're right, it should be, but it isn't and the problem is perspective.

Take a sheet of paper and hold it in front on your face... not at arms' length, but right in front of your face, two or three inches from your nose. With that perspective, the small target takes up so much of your visual space that now you can't even see the huge target – the wall – five or ten feet behind it. And the huge target is the one the represents the overall design of your life! It's really what you should be aiming for; however, until you remove the small target from your field of view, you can't even see the large target, let alone aim for it.

Think about Sam again for a minute. He was hitting all of his small targets – car, travel, house, earning more and more money from his company that grew larger and larger. Yes, he was successful with the small targets, but because he focused on those, he missed the much larger and more important target: happiness and balance in his life.

Every Human Operating System brings with it small targets as you will see, and those small targets are separate and specific to each HOS. For example, for someone with a Failure HOS, the small target is making a lot of money and climbing the ladder of success. That's the target their hijacker keeps them focused on. However, with that focus and perspective, they're missing their bigger target: time with family, fun with relationships, life with minimal stress. They keep hitting the small target over and over and put all of their energy into hitting that. Once they hit that, they self-sabotage and replace that small target with another small target like a higher and higher salary. It's simply a different version of the same thing, but it continually takes all of their emphasis and attention, so it prevents them from seeing, let alone hitting, their big target.

I want to help you understand who your hijacker is and how to program your operating system so that you can manage your mind and brainwash it as needed to help you achieve what you want out of your life – to hit your big target, to get out of your own way. One thing you should know about me is that I'm very logically minded. I think very mechanically, and I like to deliver messages in the way the mind can actually see it. It can be a challenging topic, so I will make this as tangible as possible.

Chapter Two:
The Operating Systems

While we all have a Human Operating System, there are a number of different ones. In fact, I've defined at least ten different operating systems over the years in my work with clients. Despite their differences in how they manifest in the traits and patterns that people exhibit and how they might be self-sabotaging their own efforts to achieve the life they want, every one of these operating systems works to accomplish one thing: Human Operating Systems work to cover up insecurity.

It's really rather simple: we all have insecurities. Don't be quick to dismiss that notion. Perhaps you feel like you are immune to insecurity. Or perhaps (if you're able to admit that you do have insecurities) you immediately think of someone that you know or someone famous that you believe is completely without insecurity, thinking about the way they act, what they say, and how they handle themselves. Based on their actions, you find it difficult, if not impossible, to believe that they could have any insecurities at all.

And that's exactly the point! It is their Human Operating System working full steam ahead to hide their greatest insecurity.

Once you understand the various operating systems, you'll be able to identify the one you have, and that is the first step in learning to manage it... the first step toward Conscious Discernment. By managing it, and only by managing it, can you take back control of your life...

moving the hijacker into the passenger seat and reclaiming the driver's position, so you can achieve what you want and hit your big target. So you can design the life you want and implement it. In fact, you'll likely be able to even achieve beyond what you may believe is possible at this point. Remember, the solution is inside of you, not out, and you must overcome the default programming that leads you to believe that what you want is impossible.

Operating System Development

Operating systems develop at a young age and are precipitated by a major event, usually before age seven. When I say "major event," you must keep in mind that it's relative. What is a major, defining moment to a 6-year-old, might not even register with an adult.

For some, it might be witnessing bullying or a greater level of violence over which a young child has no control. They realize at that moment, they are powerless and begin to create a story about themselves, a certain narrative, if you will. This is the germination of a Powerless operating system. Once it begins to take hold, the child begins to validate it and continues to strengthen it through other experiences.

The "major event" that spawns an operating system might be something as seemingly insignificant as not being picked for the solo in a recital or failing to get a hit in a tee-ball game. Again, keep in mind the relativity of these things to a 6-year-old. It's big stuff at that age.

You cannot prevent having an operating system in your life any more than you can prevent your computer from having an operating system and still function as it should. I assure you, as you read this, there was an event in your childhood that developed the operating system you have and have been working under your entire life. The good news is that your Human Operating System can work for you as much as it can work against you. The key is understanding what yours is and learning how to manage it. Once you accomplish that, you can use your operating system to stop self-sabotaging behavior, get out of your own way, achieve all your goals and get what you want out of life and live the life that you design for yourself.

Survival Mechanisms

While I've likened your Human Operating System to that of a computer, there is a major and fundamental difference between the two. The computer is entirely and completely objective. It carries out commands without feeling a need to survive. It is after all, mathematically based and very logical.

On the other hand, your brain, the center of your own operating system, is anything but. Sure, you can be logical at times, but in general, humans are emotional, reactive beings. It's the way we're wired. You see, most of us believe we think things through; however, the truth is that most of us are walking zombies, reacting to the world around us through our various filters. We fall under the illusion that what we see and think is the truth. I will continue to challenge this notion throughout this book.

Everything in this world has a survival mechanism. If a living being's life is threatened, it will fight for survival. Take my dogs as an example. My dogs are the best of friends; they play together, chase each other, and are each other's companion. But, if I left my dogs together in a room for two weeks without food or water, I bet I would come back to just one dog and a bloody mess. Morbid, I know. But it does illustrate how everyone and everything will fight for survival.

Now, here's the weird thing: Your operating system also has a strong survival mechanism. Believe it or not, your operating system can become threatened when challenged. If it feels threatened, it will fight for its own survival. This is the root of why we sabotage ourselves. It will fight to keep the status quo. Not so with a computer. It doesn't perceive threat and it has no survival instinct. It chugs along making the calculations it was designed to make. Humans simply don't work that way. For every operating system, when the human behind it becomes aware of how to manage it and begins to do so, the Human Operating System's survival mechanism kicks in and tries to fight for its own survival. It will attempt to affirm the insecurity behind the HOS. Bear in mind that your HOS is a significant part of your identity. When your operating system is challenged, it "fights" back to help maintain your known identity. This is critical to understand.

Your mind will find evidence for whatever it believes to be true. It will make all else an exception. Your mind will exaggerate that which supports your operating system and dismiss even the hardest, truest facts that don't support it. There is no objectivity. It's all part of its survival mechanism. It's all part of maintaining your current identity which ultimately includes perceived limits of success in business, relationships, and other accomplishments.

Operating System Overviews

Let me give you a broad overview of the various Human Operating Systems (HOS), so you begin to see where yours is and may also recognize the operating systems of others in your life as well.

Unlovable:

You might never make the connection between those with an Unlovable operating system and their actions. Unlovable HOS people are very nurturing and caring. They prefer a few very deep relationships as opposed to several more "general" friendships. I see a lot of nurses, grade school teachers, and charitable volunteers who operate under the Unlovable HOS.

Powerless:

Many presidents and those in executive positions are going through life with Powerless operating systems. Politicians striving to seek higher and higher positions? Place your bet on a Powerless HOS. But it isn't just success in business or politics. These people can be very active in physical conditioning, martial arts, or anything else that contributes to being perceived as and feeling powerful.

Incompetent:

Those with an Incompetent HOS seem to be good (if not great!) at whatever they do. Think about extraordinary athletes, like Jim Thorpe, just to name one who exceeded and worked to achieve the ultimate prize. These people are usually at the top of their game – whatever their game may be: head trainer, captain of the team, head of their class, etc.

Ugly:

When you started reading, I doubt you would have figured Marilyn Monroe as having an Ugly HOS, but I would place her in this category. Ugly people don't like to leave the house without being well manicured, made up, not a hair out of place, and perfectly coordinated. You can even spot them at the gym because their workout attire resembles that of a runway model.

Unlikeable:

If you want to better understand who is operating under an Unlikeable HOS, peruse Facebook and see who has the most friends (or most connections on LinkedIn or most followers on Twitter). Popularity comes naturally to those with this operating system. It is a by-product of their "connecting" skills. People just gravitate to those with this HOS. An Unlikeable HOS is the perfect make up for a successful salesman.

Weak:

The World's Strongest Man competition is filled with those operating under the Weak HOS, and it's not limited to the male gender. Muscles, muscles, and more muscles. They live at the gym and tout health food and other muscle-building solutions. Strength and health are paramount.

Dumb:

As you're reading through these generalized descriptions, you're quickly making the connection between the HOS classification and the opposite traits. The Dumb HOS is no exception. Dumb types often have many letters or acronyms (i.e., degrees and certifications) after their names. They like to use very big words that send the rest of us to the dictionary. When you read a book authored by someone with a Dumb HOS, you will find yourself spending as much time in the dictionary as in their book. Grade point average? 4.5, because 4.0 isn't good enough.

Outcast:

Those with an Outcast HOS are always in the mix. Their fear of missing out on… well, anything is what drives them. They are constantly on the go with a social schedule chock full of parties and gatherings. Going out is their life. Being unique is a vital element to this type. It is better to stand out than to fade into the crowd.

Failure:

Success after success defines those with the Failure HOS. People like John D. Rockefeller, who are amazing at what they can create in terms of developing and managing businesses and their success. Often Failures actually have one successful business after another.

Bad:

The person with the Bad HOS is a pleaser, and for them, every last detail has to be perfect and every rule followed to the Nth degree. There's a lot of stress for those with this HOS because perfection, though aspired by this type, is almost always impossible to achieve.

HOS Types at a Glance

Area of Dominance	HOS Type	Traits
Social Dominant	Unlikeable	Lots of friends (virtual and real world) Active social calendar Great conversationalist / "life of the party" Proverbial Sales person
	Unlovable	Caring/nurturing Self-sacrificing Generous Fewer but deeper friendships
	Bad	Rule follower "Put together" Pleaser Nice
	Outcast	Active social life Unique, stand-out traits Values individuality More unconventional

Success Dominant	Failure	Monetarily driven Desires the finer things Fancy cars, homes, watches, etc. Winning is a priority
	Powerless	High position of power Natural leader Not subservient Also likes winning
	Incompetent	Ability driven Wide range of abilities Finish on top Fiscally smart – researches all purchases
Appearance Dominant	Ugly	Perfectly "put together" Detail person Coordinator Coiffed Perfect party planner
	Weak	Strong All about physicality Fitness is a priority Uses nutritional supplements "Gym rat"

Intelligence Dominant	Dumb	Fact driven A "go-to" source for information Research-oriented Walking dictionary

Chapter Three:
Unlovable

The idea of an operating system based on being Unlovable may seem quite foreign to a lot of people, and you will be surprised at how those who deal with this particular operating system act. Outwardly, you would never make the connection between their actions and their Unlovable operating system.

Jasmine: An Unlovable

Take Jasmine. She was the softest person you could ever meet. She was nurturing and caring. Few, if any, were more thoughtful than Jasmine.

You'd be surprised to learn of the many tumultuous relationships she experienced over the course of her life. While her focus was primarily on her significant other, she didn't spend a lot of time cultivating a ton of friendships, but was very close with the few she had. That said, the deepest of those relationships could be roller coasters at times. There were times when a friend she had known since childhood, someone she'd trusted her whole life, could end up on the "outs" and on non-speaking terms as far as Jasmine was concerned.

Jasmine had a pattern: Her pattern was to love people entirely and completely until... until they did something she didn't like or felt was wrong. Until she felt slighted or betrayed (at least from her perspective) in some way. Then she could just as easily write them off completely, throw them away like used tissue. Now all of us have had disagreements – even arguments – with friends, but we usually forgive and forget, especially those with whom we've invested years, if not decades. But not Jasmine. If you crossed her, if she simply believed you did her wrong, you were no longer part of her world. You couldn't be trusted. Her emotions were more fragile than most. Despite her sweet nature, she had a very tough time maintaining lasting and meaningful relationships.

Jasmine didn't have a difficult time starting relationships. In fact, just the opposite. It was easy for people to get very close to her. She became "besties" (or best friends) with people so easily. She was the type of person people opened up to because she was so open-hearted and thoughtful. So why... why... then would she have such a tough time maintaining these relationships that started so strongly?

The answer was in her operating system. Jasmine's operating system was one of being "unlovable." When she was a young girl, her dad left her mother. As with every 5-year-old, they are the center of the universe. Everything happens because of them or for them. Although her father's departure from the house was directly related to the issues he had with Jasmine's mother, her 5-year-old mind could not comprehend that. The reason, in her mind, was because of her... because he didn't love her enough. She deemed herself unlovable.

In that moment, a mental construct was created that would continually shape Jasmine's world. From that point forward, she would gather and collect evidence that she was, in fact, unlovable. She would exaggerate any tidbit that came along that supported that belief. Anything that may have contradicted it was deemed an exception and cast aside.

But no one truly wants to be thought of as unlovable, Jasmine included, so she invested a lot of time and energy being the most loving person possible. She did for others, gave to others and was always so thoughtful of others. This endeared people to her. Friends who were going through tough times always sought Jasmine out to lean on her exceptional compassionate side

She had no idea that at the tender age of five, a mental hijacker took over her life and would stay with her forever. And since she didn't realize that the hijacker took over and was sitting in the driver's seat, she also had no idea that she could manage the hijacker. Why would she? She didn't know he existed. She lived her life only as she knew how: with him at the controls.

It wasn't until she began exploring the concept of an operating system and unraveling where hers truly took shape that she began to understand what it took to manage the hijacker and keep him in the passenger seat. Her hijacker could help her cultivate amazing relationships, but she also had to learn to discipline him to know what a long-lasting, loving relationship was really about.

Individuals with an Unlovable operating system tend to go through relationships despite their oh-so-lovable personalities. There are Unlovable types who have managed to sustain long-term marriages but with a constant sense of self-sacrifice. This continual feeling of self-sacrifice can lead to resentment. If the resentment persists too long, or is not channeled, it can become destructive to the relationship. To a degree, they also often become martyrs: They give and give until they become resentful that they're the ones giving so much, wondering why their friends and family don't reciprocate to the degree that they do. All the while, their friends and family are unaware of the Unlovable's needs, given they are not the type to communicate their own needs – that feels too "selfish." Communicating needs would make them feel unlovable. They generally don't address their feelings of resentment, and since they never communicate those feelings, they fester like an unattended cancer. Growing and growing and growing, until the disease has taken such a strong hold, that it feels impossible to fix or repair the damage.

They don't do anything until it has gone too far... until it reaches the point at which they can't take it anymore. Then they explode. It very much becomes the situation of "the straw that broke the camel's back." Their reaction comes as a surprise to everyone around them. The emotions become forceful, the resentment so strong that it seems like this person is "not even themselves." Those on the receiving end don't know how to relate to "this" person. This person is not who they know. This expressed communication of what had been suppressed inside – when it finally happens – seems to come out of left field, and those to whom it is directed are often at a loss of how to respond or react. This expression can lead to confusion and further misunderstanding. Frequently, once an Unlovable has gotten to this point, the repairs become twice as difficult to make. To further complicate things, the significant other now has their own feelings of resentment for being made "wrong" for something they never even knew they were doing, not doing, saying, not saying, etc.

because the Unlovable never communicated these needs along the way.

The way out of this quagmire is for both people to realize this vulnerability in the Unlovable and for the Unlovable to take responsibility for the fact that they are now communicating things that have been pent up for too long. They both need to understand and recognize that each of them has needs and desires, and the only way to work it out is through communication... communication that comes out of the commitment each of them has to a strong and meaningful relationship.

The road to becoming self-expressed is a challenging one for the Unlovable – and even for those around them. The change feels so drastic that it seems as though it is a new relationship. One that requires a lot of work and even more understanding and forgiveness. Understanding each other's needs and forgiving one another for being human, for doing the best that each of them knows how to do. Then to move on toward the commitment of an even deeper relationship.

Career Tendencies

Keep in mind that each operating system can have its benefits as well as its challenges, and those benefits may manifest in career choices and advancement.

The Unlovable can succeed in a number of vocations, especially where there is a requirement to tend to others' needs. They quickly become a trusted source because of their willingness to "self-sacrifice." Careers that involve being a service to others, where caring and nurturing are high priorities are great places for those with an Unlovable operating system to succeed.

Teachers, nurses, doctors, counselors, therapists and other various advisors are common careers where you can find successful Unlovables.

It is vital for Unlovables to understand that their care-taking nature, while it is a tremendous strength, can also become a source of "burn out" unless they tend to their own needs to refuel their "personal tanks," if you will. As with the example of Jasmine in her personal relationships, an Unlovable can fail to communicate the need for a break until it becomes too much and potentially too late. The Unlovable must understand that communicating that need is entirely okay and does not make them an unlovable person.

Highlights of an Unlovable:

- They are self-sacrificers and very nurturing.
- They may go through a few tumultuous relationships.
- See themselves as the martyr and have a constant sense of giving so much, but not getting much in return.
- Avoid communicating their needs.
- Feelings of resentment are a challenge.
- Excel as caregivers.

Outward actions/appearances:

- Loving and nurturing personality.
- Deep relationships that may turn tumultuous or be completely abandoned when the Unlovable feels slighted.

- Starts relationships easily but struggles to balance giving so much of themselves with less reciprocation.
- Martyr syndrome: Continually giving to the relationship until the Unlovable develops resentment about being "the one who's always giving."

Possible precipitating event:

A divorce or other similar rift in a family is the most typical precipitating event when a young child believes that they are the cause.

Small Target Issues:

- Intense focus on pleasing people – giving of themselves to others.
- Energy spent on developing relationships.

Unlovable

Chapter Four:
Powerless

As you're no doubt seeing by now, the designation of the operating system and the traits exhibited by those with that particular operating system are 180 degrees apart from each other. Very, very true with the Powerless Human Operating System.

John is a great example of someone operating with a Powerless HOS. He exudes tremendous confidence and has a commanding presence. You notice when John enters the room. Since developing his Powerless operating system, he has never been one to be the meek one in the room. Even without speaking, you get a sense of John's desire to prove that he is in charge.

He wears a big watch that complements his broad stature. He drives a big truck and owns a big dog – not just any big dog, a mastiff – one of the very biggest of big dogs. John has a black belt in Jujitsu and works very hard to maintain his level of fitness. It probably won't surprise you to learn that he also is the CEO of the company he created and is very comfortable being the star of the show.

As one with a Powerless HOS, John needs to continually prove just how powerful he is and that he is always in charge. While that may seem a bit self-serving, his actual mission is to ensure that he can not only take care of himself but that he can make sure those around him are safe as well. That mission is directly related to the precipitating event that created his HOS.

In many cases, the instigation for a Powerless HOS may be more traumatic than those that create some of the other operating systems. That was John's experience as a 6-year-old. After the end of a party in the house late at night, John heard a ruckus and left his bedroom to see what was going on. He crept into the kitchen and what he saw was his father pinning his mother against the wall – a case of domestic violence. His reaction was to come to his mother's aid and stop what was happening. His father's reaction to his attempted interference was to swat him aside, knocking him to the floor. In that moment, John declared himself powerless and his HOS was formed.

He created a narrative about his place in the world. He was a powerless little kid who created a story of being a powerless adult. Keep in mind that the precipitating event for the HOS is never conscious at the moment it occurs. It is only until we look back that we can begin to recognize those moments that created deep sear marks (or imprints) on our brain. You might not be able to immediately draw a line from one event experienced as a child to your operating system, but once you do uncover it, you will be able to recall that event with vivid detail.

From that moment in the kitchen late at night forward, John did things that helped him maintain a position of power, including playing hockey and football in school. He gravitated toward contact sports as do many with this operating system. Powerless people (generally male, but not always) need to prove over and over and over just how powerful they are. They don't play subordinate roles in their careers; they're the CEOs and managers, executives and "head honchos." Many U.S. presidents have had Powerless operating systems. In their careers, the Powerless have to climb to the top and go as high as they can. They're highly competitive and like to be better than others. One upping those around them is normal course of business. Military careers or aspirations to be in the military are also a common trait in this group.

Faster, Stronger, Better

Like John, those with a Powerless HOS are generally physically fit because fitness represents another element of power – being faster and stronger than the next guy and being faster, stronger, and fitter than they were yesterday. In addition to fitness, their salaries are another power tool. Earning more elevates their position of power. The importance of finances in their lives is a higher salary and a bigger bottom line.

Having a Powerless HOS – and being unaware of it – can present some huge hurdles in relationships. It is difficult, almost impossible, for a Powerless person to be subservient. Let me reiterate that the Powerless individual equates being in charge with providing security to his family and those around him. To him, it's a good thing! Subservience is weakness; weakness is insecurity. On the flip side, it often creates a lot of power struggles inside relationships until there is a better understanding of operating systems and how to manage them.

If the partner or spouse of the Powerless person doesn't require the perceived level of security, there's going to be a clash. Someone who likes to be an equal is a true challenge to a Powerless person. It's a threat to their operating system because the operating system is working to hide insecurities – remembering (consciously or not) the inciting incident of true powerlessness as a child. They will never allow themselves to be put in a "helpless" situation again.

The partner or spouse may struggle to get a Powerless to "open up" and be "vulnerable." These are two words or phrases that make an unconscious Powerless wince. To be emotionally accessible requires work and commitment on the part of someone with this HOS. When partnered with someone who requires a great deal of independence and has confidence can often be seen as a threat. Why? Remember, the mission of the Powerless is to protect the other, so you can see that a partner or spouse who doesn't need protection creates a real conflict.

Now, bear in mind, these descriptions and traits under each chapter describing the various operating systems are common traits when left unconscious and not dealt with or addressed. Many people have undergone a great amount of personal work, therapy, personal and/or business coaching, training in a martial arts, etc. These can slightly adjust the extreme levels of each operating system, but nonetheless, the traits or tendencies still exist – like a persistent itch that just won't go away.

As mentioned previously, those with a Powerless HOS thrive when others follow them. They know how to align the troops which also makes them very powerful enrollers. This trait allows them to succeed in executive positions as it is a vital skill set to a leader to enroll those around him in a vision.

Once John learned who his hijacker was, he was able to better manage it. With knowledge of his operating system, he's more able to rein in his need to be in charge with his family and those around him and channel that need more appropriately – on the playing field, in the gym, in the boardroom. He was able to leverage his HOS to work for him and create a great level of success for him and his family.

Highlights of a Powerless:

- They crave positions of power.
- Not only do they crave position of power, they *thrive* in positions of power.
- Vulnerability is a challenge for Powerless.
- Commanding the troops is where they excel. Great leaders are often a result of this HOS.
- Personal/family security is a top priority.

Outward actions/appearances:

- Very confident, commanding personalities.
- Wants to prove they're in charge.
- Likes "big": big car, big jewelry, big dog, etc.
- Ongoing desire to display power: managers, CEOs, presidents, military higher ranks.
- Gravitates toward physical fitness; contact sports.
- Tends to be male oriented but not exclusively.
- Rarely subservient in relationships.

Possible precipitating event:

May be more traumatic than in other HOS types (being struck, abuse, bullied, etc.)

Small Target Issues:

- Climbing the career ladder simply to reach the top (may not derive any job satisfaction at lower levels; too fixated on the next level).
- Focus on being better, fitter, etc. than yesterday (perceived power improvement).
- Anything competitive.

Chapter Five:
Incompetent

The very simple definition of "incompetent" is not having or showing the necessary skills to do something successfully. For those with an Incompetent operating system, they not only have the necessary skills to do *something* successfully, they strive to do nearly *everything* successfully. Successfully, perfectly, extraordinarily well. Well, except for those things they can't do well right off the bat (I'll explain later).

Let me start with a story, my story. I have to confess that I run on an Incompetent operating system. Before I tell my story, I need to reiterate that the precipitating event may seem entirely silly to an adult when viewed in retrospect with years of adult understanding under our belts; however, it is critically important to remember that these events are experienced by young children. It is vital to understand that it is the feeling at the time that becomes embedded in a young brain and lingers there forever, like a bruise that doesn't heal. Each time that bruise is touched, that sensitivity further reinforces the operating system.

So with that said:

As a young child, I had a very close best friend. Annette lived next door, and we did everything together. We dressed alike and participated in activities together. Whatever Annette did, I did and vice versa. Our moms even enrolled us in dance class together. I agreed to participate because Annette was going to get involved.

Annette's mother was a dancer herself. They even created a studio in their basement.

My participation in dance class was for fun and to be with my friend. I didn't practice every day, but Annette was far more regimented and did. She was a year older than I was and more advanced and better practiced than me. I clearly recall the day in class at the dance studio when we were preparing for the year-end recital. Someone was going to be announced as the solo act. The instructor went on for several minutes describing the honor of being the soloist and continuing to build up its importance. A group of about 14 young 5-year-olds stood in eager anticipation. As you can probably guess, when she announced the name of the year's most important role of soloist, it wasn't mine; it was Annette's. Annette had no doubt earned it; however, in that moment, I saw that I wasn't good enough. I wasn't competent enough for the coveted role. And in that moment, my Incompetent HOS was formed. I admit that it seems a bit unimportant all these years later, but in that moment, I was devastated. Even to this day, feelings of being incompetent still creep up inside.

My mission then became to prove that I was, indeed, highly competent. I wasn't very athletic and not good at sports... I couldn't get over my fear of injury. I tried soccer and t-ball (like a lot of little kids), but I quit because my fear of getting hurt didn't allow me to be aggressive and to excel. On the other hand, when I discovered things for which I had some level of skill, I would focus on being *the best* at each and every one of them. For me, this was particularly true in academics.

A basic college degree wasn't good enough for me. My goals required advanced degrees. I was the youngest one in my master's degree program. I took a lot of pride in that distinction. It wasn't a matter of graduating – it was a matter of graduating at the top of my class. While putting myself through school, I became one of top two recognized therapists for autistic children in San Diego, and my focus was on proving how good a therapist I was.

After completing my master's degree, and at the young age of 24, I started working as a coach for a training and development company. I was by far the youngest employee of the company. My aspirations were to become the *head coach*, to create the coaching curriculum, to train all the other coaches, and to travel the country speaking and training like the senior people I worked with. Within six months, I'd achieved all of these goals… and again, was proud of it.

I wasn't climbing to the top (as someone would who operates with a Powerless HOS would). I was climbing not to prove that I was powerful and in charge – I didn't have an interest in being a leader – but rather, I was climbing to prove that I was the best at what I did. This is an important distinction between the Incompetent and the Powerless. My successfulness was tangible proof that I was not incompetent.

Research and Control

Those with Incompetent operating systems are well-prepared for whatever they are going into and pursuing. Their biggest fear is screwing up (aka being incompetent), so they study new information wholeheartedly. If you know an Incompetent, you know that they are the ones who research ev-er-y-thing before acting.

Control freak? Possibly someone with an Incompetent HOS. They enjoy being in charge of their outcomes and having things turn out the way they want them to.

Outwardly, Incompetents like to show that they know what they are doing. They don't drive the most expensive cars, but neither do they drive beaters. Their cars reflect that they have things under control. An Incompetent would never take on a huge, unaffordable car payment just to show off a flashy, expensive car – that is left for a different HOS.

Their financial lives run a parallel course – they're usually financially successful regardless of what their salaries may be. Even in careers that don't typically pay well, Incompetents will have financial success because they are very diligent about money management. For them, being broke equals being incompetent.

Relationships for a person with an Incompetent operating system are usually healthy, or at least they appear that way. A failed relationship is not something they would want to expose. If they do, it was clearly the other person's fault.

However, people with this HOS also have a strong need to be right... all the time. This is a trait that doesn't serve most relationships well. If the partner of an Incompetent is a person who likes others to take control and have the other person be the one to figure things out and manage them... well, that sounds like a match made in heaven.

On the other hand, if that partner is insecure, they can feel very threatened by an Incompetent. If they're not completely secure, being with an Incompetent can be challenging. Those going through life with an Incompetent HOS also take on a lot and do it themselves, often under the mindset: If you want anything done right, do it yourself. Problems arise because the Incompetent can begin to feel animosity against those around them because they're the ones "doing everything" without recognizing that it is self-inflicted.

Several years ago, we bought a 40-foot motor home, and as an Incompetent, I read all of the manuals. I figured I had to master it... and there were dozens of manuals for every system it had: the engine, the slides, the power exhaust system, and yes, even the septic system! Driving it was another challenge. We had a long, steep driveway that we needed to back this "bus" into. I was convinced I had to be able to back it into the driveway and park it. My husband (who's a Powerless HOS) didn't want me to attempt it. In his mind, he was protecting me; in my mind, he thought I was incompetent. This was just another thing I had to master. On the other hand, his Powerless HOS believed that I felt he was not able to handle such a big, powerful machine.

Two completely different narratives for the same situation based on each of our differing HOS types. What had the potential to become a major, drawn out battle lasted just a few short minutes because we were each aware of our own operating systems and how their inclinations affect us. We were both able to recognize that we were falling into a familiar pattern and stop ourselves before our unconscious minds took over. Unfortunately for most couples, they don't even know they have an HOS, let alone how it impacts the relationship. So many relationships end prematurely, not because the partners are not good people and not even because they don't want what is best for the relationship (at least consciously), but because of their blind spots... because of what they don't know they don't know about themselves and their partners – the core system that has each of them understand the world and their place in it.

Understanding your HOS and the HOS's of those around you, helps to resolve misunderstandings before they become big issues.

Careers

The Incompetents can be found in several different vocations. You will find them in a wide variety of careers, though they typically gravitate to respected careers; ones that reflect their ability and their efforts. They are great at making things happen and happen at a "competent" level. You want Incompetents to work for you – especially if you enjoy having the confidence that things will get done right. They may inadvertently take control of the office, the team, a project, etc., but you won't have to worry about it not getting done in true competent fashion.

Differentiation

Dumb and Failure are two HOS's that are related to the Incompetent, but distinct. The difference with an Incompetent is that they are accepting of the fact that someone else can be smarter so long as they feel they can carry on an intellectual conversation competently with their

Dumb counterpart. Incompetents don't need to use the biggest words, and they don't feel the need to educate others on historical facts; they just need to feel they are very capable.

Failures and Incompetents are also very similar. The difference here is that Failures have a need to show, illustrate, and display monetary success. While Incompetents take pride in their financial successes, they are not consumed by having the biggest house, the most expensive car, or even the most attractive spouse. Like most things, Incompetents' ability to have their finances in control keeps these desires in check.

Highlights:

- Incompetents pick and choose where they apply themselves.
- They set themselves up to be proficient.
- They are researchers and like to have all the information and facts before acting.
- They have a need to be right.
- They have a desire to be in control.
- They are great at managing several things at once – think air traffic controller.

Outward actions/appearances:

- Strive to be good, if not great, at everything, but will avoid activities/tasks at which they cannot excel.
- Status quo isn't good enough (e.g. will pursue advanced degrees and work to be at the top of the class).

- Aspirations to exceed are driven by the Incompetent's need to prove they are not incompetent (not to reach the top [e.g. Powerless trait]).
- Tend to be control freaks.
- Regardless of salary, they are financially successful.
- Choice of car reflects that they're in control (e.g. won't buy more than they can afford), but will tend to have a vehicle that exemplifies the fact that they are better than most at what they do.
- "If I want it done right, do it myself" mentality.

Possible precipitating event:

Sense of not being the best at something (e.g., not chosen for a special role, not winning the spelling bee, failing at a task or skill).

Small Target Issue:

- Constant pursuit of academic degrees (or similar success) simply to be able to point to the achievement.
- Intense focus to master "the next thing" whatever it may be.

Chapter Six:
Ugly

Do you know the person who is always, and I mean *always*, put together and perfectly coordinated? Everything matches and accessories always complement the clothing? The person who makes you feel dowdy and maybe even inspires you to take a second look in the mirror before meeting her for lunch? The sports bra (whether or not it's seen) matches the tennis shoes? A shoe collection that rivals or possibly exceeds Imelda Marco? Yeah, that person.

I guarantee this type of person is being controlled by an Ugly operating system. Their looks are their top priority, and they would never consider even stepping out of the house to get the newspaper or mail unless they were completely put together.

Let me tell you about Naomi. Naomi is, without a doubt, a naturally beautiful woman. Perfect complexion, perfect hair. She is even stunning without make up. However, Naomi doesn't see that. She came from Japan as a young child, and her family settled into an area that did not include other Japanese families. Naomi was the only one who looked like she did in her neighborhood and school. While the other kids fully accepted her, her looks – that of being so different – created a deep-seated insecurity and subsequently her Ugly HOS. No matter that she dressed and acted like her friends, she was still obviously different.

With her Ugly hijacker in control, Naomi spends, spends, and spends on her looks. She has her nails done every week (whether or not it's really needed) and also has a weekly salon appointment. She considers her aesthetician and hair dresser to be her best friends, and they probably know her better than other people. Because they're a very important part of her world, her generosity toward them at the holidays is almost unprecedented. In fact, she "invests" so much with them, they should be buying *her* gifts during the holiday season.

Her wardrobe is extensive – to the point that Naomi probably doesn't repeat an outfit in several weeks, if not months. On top of that, she has earrings perfectly matched to every outfit. Ditto for shoes. The most important room in her house? You guessed it – her closet. She is well aware of all of the latest styles, not allowing anything in her closet that is out of date. With as put together and coordinated as the Uglies are on the outside, no one would guess that there is a war raging inside. Getting ready for an event is an event in itself. It can cause great stress in their world because not being well put together means not fitting in properly. This discomfort can even lead them to leave an event early or not go at all.

Many of Naomi's relationship problems stem from the amount of time she spends to get ready. Her makeup regimen alone takes almost an hour. Choosing her clothing and doing her hair adds to that. It becomes a point of contention with her husband because they are always running late for events, and he doesn't understand the need for all the extra attention since he recognizes her beauty without the additional effort. Her friends know she will never arrive on time for anything. Consider this occurrence for Naomi: After spending two hours in her closet looking for the right thing to wear, and at her husband's urging to make a decision, she chose an outfit... but it didn't feel quite right to her. While at her friend's party, she felt so insecure about her looks that she ended up leaving the event early because she felt, well, ugly. Reality: nothing could have been further from the truth.

Out of Place

Feeling ugly means feeling out of place. When not properly put together, Uglies believe they stick out like a sore thumb.

I assure you, there are plenty of people (predominantly women) whose lives are dictated by their Ugly operating systems, regardless of their ethnic backgrounds. They are truly beautiful people, and no one would ever think of them as anything short of beautiful, let alone ugly. The Uglies make decisions based on the impact it will have on their looks and their ability to maintain their appearances. Like Naomi, these people may even make a real estate purchase decision based solely on the closet space. It is simply their priority. In addition to artwork and photos hanging on the walls, they'll have a lot of mirrors in the house.

Another trait of an Ugly (one often envied by others), is their ability to coordinate – not just outfits, but events as well. You know you have arrived at a party hosted by an Ugly when you walk through the door and it feels like you just walked into a Martha Stewart magazine. Every detail is perfect and well thought out. It is not just that the cups match the plates, but there is a theme running through every fine detail. From the floating flowers in the pool to the coordinated lights and even the shape of the ice cubes. Their ability to consider all the fine details make them ideal event coordinators, party planners, flower arrangers, etc.

The Uglies typically drive pretty cars, usually of European design with sleek lines and elegant interiors. The car's function is to reinforce or enhance their overall appearance; its performance is secondary. In continually surrounding themselves with pretty things, people with this HOS also like to have pretty friends. Opting for cosmetic surgical procedures is also another typical trait of an Ugly, but that is certainly not limited to this group.

In terms of finances, the Uglies are less concerned. Money is only a function of making themselves and their surroundings beautiful. In some cases, it requires a lot of money, so these folks may choose to marry accordingly. Higher education isn't a priority. Certainly there are intelligent Uglies with degrees, but it isn't a primary driver for them.

The Ugly operating system can actually bring a couple together. After all, spouses of Uglies remain attracted to them long term, but money can become a later source of contention. They can't see eye-to-eye on spending so much money on her looks when she is naturally beautiful. The husband can't comprehend why it's necessary, and the Ugly doesn't understand how her husband can fail to see its critical importance. She begins to feel as though her husband doesn't appreciate the time it takes to be "presentable." And like Naomi's situation, fights over simply getting ready and leaving the house on time become a constant.

In relationships outside of a marriage or partnership, the Uglies, while surrounding themselves with pretty friends, typically evaluate others on their looks and how pretty their stuff is. For those with an Ugly HOS, their need and desire to surround themselves with beautiful people can trigger their most sensitive insecurity. Their need to stand out physically can be compromised when their friends are also well put together. An internal struggle ensues – the need to be surrounded by pretty people yet being surrounded by pretty people can conjure up feelings of not being "as pretty." This serves to reinforce the insecure feeling and, therefore, the identity of the individual.

When an identity of an individual is threatened, a survival mechanism kicks in. That survival mechanism struggles to maintain status quo – to perpetuate the very identity that gives them "a place in the world." Just when an Ugly is feeling great about their fit body, perfect outfit, and new hair color, along comes their best friend who just had a facelift and looks 10 years younger.

Highlights:

- Uglies are some of the most attractive, well put together people.
- They make tremendous event coordinators due to their attention to detail.
- Their world looks perfectly put together.
- The attractions in their relationships are usually sustained long term.

- Their relationships challenges may stem from spending time and money on appearances. Why does an outfit or party need to cost so much?

Outward actions/appearances:

- Always perfectly coordinated.
- Extensive wardrobe with matching accessories.
- Spends extraordinarily on anything that improves outward appearance (e.g. nail and hair salons, etc.).
- Time spent on looks is paramount, usually to the point of tardiness in almost all other aspects of an Ugly's life.
- Tends to be female oriented but not exclusively.
- Money is only important because it serves as a means to make themselves beautiful.

Possible precipitating event:

Sense of not looking like other children (e.g. Ugly may stand out ethnically in neighborhood or school, not having enough money for being dressed like the other kids).

Small Target Issues:

- Need to update wardrobe to the latest fashions.
- Constant energy spent on being "the most beautiful."
- Every detail matters – hyper-attention to coordinating events.

Chapter Seven:
Unlikeable

Think of the person who seems to have a million friends. They tend to be flocked by people they know when they go out for an evening. Each time they are out in public, someone they know inevitably finds them. Everyone knows one of these types. I personally encounter Unlikeables on a consistent basis as this type often finds themselves in sales positions. For this person, with an Unlikeable hijacker at the controls, as long as they're having fun, all is good. It's all a party.

These folks have a thousand friends, and that's not simply a reflection of virtual friends on social media. Sure, the Unlikeables may have astronomical numbers of virtual friends, but they also have a huge number of actual friends. People gravitate toward them, and they are the ones who are often coordinating the events, activities, and parties. It's quite common to find Unlikeables as the presidents of fraternities, sororities, or other similar social organizations.

Take Randy, for example. He was, in fact, the president of his fraternity and has carried his penchant for a party well into adulthood. He's very involved in social media, and his Facebook posts are always exuding fun, fun, and more fun. Every weekend, he's posting photos of gatherings with his friends… watching the big game together, playing golf, outings with family along with several friends and their families, the community block party that he organized, and the list goes on and on.

During the week, he's active on LinkedIn connecting others. As with most people of this type, Randy is a connector at heart. He takes a lot of pride in creating success for others by creating mutually beneficial relationships. People appreciate that... and *like* Randy for it. People like and appreciate Unlikeables for several reasons, but perhaps the most common reason is that Unlikeables simply make people feel good about themselves. They make them feel important and wanted. They make others feel the way that they want to feel. As a result, they make things happen – for themselves *and* for others. Is there such a thing as "happening-makers?" If so, it's the Unlikeables.

It may not surprise you to learn that Randy is a sales executive and thrives on being in front of people and solving their problems. When not face-to-face with clients, he's on the phone always working to provide value for the relationship. He adds his clients to his list of friends, and it's not at all unusual for him to socialize with them outside of their professional environment. Some business professionals don't believe in mixing business with pleasure – Unlikeables don't know any other way of being.

Pros and Cons

This is a tremendous asset to individuals in relationship-based sales. When I work with individuals with Unlikeable operating systems, it's easy to get them to do relationship-building activities, whereas with other types, it is often a constant struggle that requires some creative coaching. Don't get me wrong, the best asset of Unlikeables can also bring along its challenges. Their main challenge typically revolves around over-extending themselves. They don't want to miss out on any event or opportunity and they don't want to say no to friends and clients.

This can lead them into the great challenge commonly known in the training industry as "Time Management." In my opinion, time management is a bit of a misnomer. More accurately, it is "Priority Management." Unlikeables have a difficult challenge in managing their priorities because many of their priorities conflict with one another. Serving their clients is important, serving their family is important, meeting their sales goals is important to make their managers and their spouses happy… on and on…. This, as you might imagine creates internal conflicts for Unlikeables.

Randy's Unlikeable operating system is the result of being the younger sibling of a very accomplished older brother. When he started kindergarten, he was not as advanced as his older brother was at that age, and the comparisons began in earnest. His older brother always did very, very well academically, and Randy always heard about his brother's success. Since they attended the same school and were only a few years apart, Randy often had teachers who had also had his brother in class. While teachers' comparisons were often a figment of his imagination, they were very real to Randy.

He quickly learned at a young age that his ability to get a laugh also got him attention. He might not have been as book smart as his older brother, but his antics and sense of humor drew others to him. He realized that this was how he could fit in. He may not have been as smart as his brother, but he was far funnier… and people loved that. His ability to be the center of attention became his driver and hijacked his life.

From grade school on, Randy felt an intrinsic reward by making others laugh and by helping them in some way. He found this was how he stood out from his brother. He appreciated being known for something his brother was not. He began to focus more and more of his attention on doing those things that cultivated his friendships – helping (and entertaining) others.

Aside from being able to spot Unlikeables by the number of friends on their Facebook pages, you can also spot them on the road driving more "reasonable" cars. You see, driving a flashy car tends to put your success in others' faces – an undesirable trait to this type. So Unlikeables avoid doing so. They prefer the more understated vehicle. It may be a higher level brand if they are successful but certainly not anything too flashy.

Unlikeables may or may not be financially successful. If they are, it is likely to be the result of their ability to cultivate relationships – getting others to like them. Regardless, they tend to spend quite a bit on entertaining and don't hesitate to pick up the tab. This tendency can create serious financial problems if they don't have the discretionary income to support it.

However, on the other hand, if an Unlikeable is in a career that depends on this operating system, it can really work to their benefit. Sales and entertainment are two industries in which an Unlikeable can be very financially successful and command a substantial salary. They also make good bartenders or restaurant owners because they're great at making others feel good about themselves! That's the key to good tips and devoted customers. These folks create value by entertaining. When was the last time you encountered a meek and mild sales rep who was extraordinarily successful?

Unlikeable vs. Unlovable

It may start to get a little confusing if you are considering the differences between Unlikeables and Unlovables, but there is a clear distinction between the two. For the Unlikeable, the thing that matters most is their number of friendships. They'll have a thousand friends. On the other hand, Unlovables will have far fewer relationships, but they are much, much deeper. For the Unlikeable, the majority of their relationships may only be skin deep, and if they part ways, no problem – there will be another friend around the corner who comes along to fill the vacancy. Unlovables never see their relationships as disposable. Unlovables will put themselves last in their relationships; Unlikeables are not quite as self-sacrificing.

In terms of more intimate relationships, things can go pretty smoothly as long as Unlikeables don't forgo the relationship for their social life. When both partners welcome a non-stop social life, chock full of events, activities, and late-night parties, it works. It becomes problematic when the social life comes before the spouse and the family. When the spouse says, "I wish we could just have one quiet night in," or if a spouse begins to feel the Unlikeable is spending more of their attention helping and supporting the lives of his friends while ignoring the needs of their spouse, those could be red flags for trouble.

Unlikeables spend a lot of time paying attention to other people and their experiences. This can quickly become a hurdle if that level of attention is perceived to exceed the level of attention paid to a spouse.

The Unlikeable OS formed to let the person become the center of attention. As we have mentioned, Unlikeables are very good at making others feel good about themselves. They entertain and recognize first when someone needs a refill on their drink. That said, Unlikeables want to be adored back. This can also become a relationship hurdle. If the Unlikeable isn't feeling appreciated, he or she may seek it from a new relationship. As long as you illustrate your appreciation to an Unlikeable, things are all good.

Potential for Serious Consequences

One of the biggest downsides to the Unlikeable OS is that these people may compromise themselves in order to be liked by others. Although it's rare, they may even compromise their core values for the attention and adoration. This is another distinction between Unlikeables and Unlovables. The latter would never make this sort of compromise. They may make other compromises in putting others before themselves but typically not to the point of compromising a core value.

Compromising a core value can lead to much more devastating issues. When an Unlikeable goes this far and elects to compromise that which is ingrained and critically important to them in order to be liked or even adored, it creates a confusing struggle between two very deep-seated factors: the need to entertain and a core value. Both are important to the Unlikeable, and they may literally not be able to live with themselves as a result of this level of compromise.

Additionally, when taken to an extreme (and I mean ***real*** extreme), some Unlikeables may even feel empty inside. They may start to feel that those around them are "using" them for what they provide them: contacts, free meals, free entertainment. A deep-seated consternation can arise when this happens. They may even question their worth outside of "bribing" their friends. When you think about some of the biggest celebrities who have committed suicide unexpectedly, I'm willing to bet many of them had an Unlikeable OS. This tragic result comes as a surprise to the general public because the internal struggle is well hidden by an Unlikeable. A perfect example: the numerous comedians we lost to suicide; all smiles on the outside, but a real emptiness inside. Sharing this information would tend to repel not attract people, so the hijacker in the Unlikeable's life would never allow them to reveal this struggle and confusion. They sadly but literally can't live with themselves.

However, if an Unlikeable succeeds at marrying their values with their social life, they lead extremely successful, balanced and highly rewarding lives.

Highlights of an Unlikeable:

- They have a vast social life.
- They need to be adored.
- They know how to make others feel special.
- They can throw a last minute party with 100 of their "closest friends."

- They excel in sales and other relationship-based industries.
- Their friendships may be disposable.

Outward actions/appearances:

- Life of the party.
- Hundreds of friends (may be thousands of friends in the virtual world); friendships aren't very deep.
- Unlikeables are the event coordinators (president of fraternity/sorority or social/civic organizations).
- Likes to have fun and be adored.
- Avoids flashy cars and other trappings that flaunt success (people dislike that trait, and Unlikeables are sensitive to that).
- Not necessarily financially successful but quick to pick up the tab.

Possible precipitating event:

Being in the shadow of someone else, i.e., a successful sibling (Unlikeable learns that humor/class clown approach becomes the way to fit in).

Small Target Issues:

- Continually adding friends (either real or online), and needing to keep up with staying connected to them.
- Energy spent on coordinating the next party, event, etc.

Chapter Eight:
Weak

Perhaps you picture the 98-pound weakling as the prototype for the Weak operating system. You may picture a scrawny, pale stick-like figure, and although that may be the foundation for this HOS, it manifests itself as the total opposite of this image. Instead, picture the body builder with large muscles – Charles Atlas, if you will – and you will be picturing the archetypical (albeit stereotypical) guy with a Weak operating system.

I say "guy" because this operating system truly tends to be male dominated. It's not impossible for a woman to be weak, but statistically, less likely.

Zack's operating system is Weak. He's not the tallest guy you'll meet, but he may be the most muscular. Zack is a personal trainer which is a perfect career for him: He gets to spend all day in the gym, which feels like a second home, *and* he gets paid for it. His favorite workout is based on strength training. It would be atypical to find a man with the Weak HOS running every day. Running (and other aerobic, heavy cardio workouts like swimming or cycling) make you lean which is not the objective of the Weak HOS. The objective of the Weak's endeavors is strength… and muscles. Before landing the job as a trainer, he was spending three to four hours every day at the gym working out anyway. Since high school, his passion and focus has been on developing his physique, but Zack isn't doing so for just the wellness benefit. In fact, his time spent on his body truly transcends what is needed for health and wellness. You also wouldn't want to mess with someone who is Weak. They are quick to defend themselves and others. They don't hesitate to use their strength to resolve problems.

Have you been to a bar lately where they check your I.D. at the door? If not, remember back to the last time you had to hand your state license over before entering. What did the guy (aka, the bouncer) look like? Ninety-nine percent of the time, it's a guy with giant muscles who looks like he could lift you with his pinky finger... and very possibly could do just that. You just encountered someone who is proving to the world he is **not** weak.

As I alluded to earlier, HOS types are created when we're young children, and Zack is no different. Zack was the perfect target for bullies as a young boy. He was always the smallest one from the time he entered kindergarten. Always relegated to the front row of the class picture (and sometimes the only boy to be in that position). Always needed help to reach things. An easy target. He was an average student and did not stand out as the smartest or funniest one. Zack resented the treatment, and the Weak hijacker took over control of his life before he entered first grade.

In addition to his job as a trainer, Zack sells a line of supplements. His interest in this isn't necessarily the additional income the sales create. For Zack, his product sales help offset his own use of the products. He's constantly touting them because he's always taking them. He is "living proof" that they are effective (never mind the hours of heavy lifting he does daily). He's convinced they are helping him develop greater muscle density, definition, and strength. You and I may not notice the subtle difference, but he clearly does. He is the perfect representative for the supplements he sells since he certainly epitomizes the results the products *promise*. His interest in athletic competition is in the realm of body building rather than a discipline that focuses on other athletic talents such as speed, skill, or stamina.

Zack is very typical of the Weak HOS. Because these guys invest so much time cultivating their physique, they don't generally spend a lot of time cultivating other areas of their lives. More time and energy are spent on building themselves physically than on any other area of their lives including intellectual and social development. Their social world is primarily comprised of other "gym rats," the ones they see regularly at their favorite haunt.

Distinction: Weak vs. Powerless

Watch who climbs out of a truck which has been raised three or four feet off the ground… there is a very high probability it is a guy with *a lot* of muscles. Like those with a Powerless HOS, the Weak drive trucks, Hummers, SUVs – big, strong, manly vehicles – never something sleek or elegant. But that is where the similarity between a Weak and a Powerless ends. The Powerless individual is looking to get ahead while the Weak looks to overpower or defend. It would be common to find Weaks as body guards or in the military.

For the Powerless, their motivation is to climb to the top, and as athletes, they are driven by competitive factors rather than mere muscle size. The Powerless understand that muscular strength is a means to an end:

winning. For the Weak, muscular strength and showing it off is the end in and of itself. While not guaranteed, it would not be unlikely for those with Weak operating systems to be steroid users, enjoying the muscular bulk that comes with it. That's certainly not to say that all steroid users have a Weak HOS or that everyone with a Weak HOS is a steroid user! What I am saying is that it never surprises me to discover a link between the two when it does occur. And in full transparency, I don't coach too many clients with Weak operating systems because they don't tend to reach out for personal "help." Help is a sign of weakness. Their primary focus is building physical strength.

That is another distinction between Powerless and Weak: Whereas, a Weak may use supplements to get ahead, a Powerless will spend quite a lot of time reading and researching how to gain more power, whether it is physical power or power climbing the ranks in their respective fields. They want to be at the top in competition and in their careers. On the other hand, there is no specific financial definition for the Weak. They often have average incomes. Their attention is not on career success; it's on getting stronger and on doing things that exhibit their physical strength. However, this does play well into careers in which physical strength is an attribute.

In relationships, the Weak may find challenges because they are often not emotionally vulnerable since the precipitating event that causes this operating system is usually one of being bullied. They use physicality to wall themselves off from other feelings. That figurative wall tends to create other relationship obstacles. Allowing themselves to be vulnerable in a relationship, to show feelings, may also allow themselves to be hurt... and that would obviously be unacceptable. They illustrate that they care about another by seeing themselves as a protector. Do not mess with the significant other of a Weak. They will not hesitate to put you in your place.

Someone with a Weak HOS would be well served to recognize that their strength is their strength (sorry for the unintended pun) and health. They should pay attention and begin to manage the challenges that can arise with higher levels of testosterone. Not allowing others to "get their goat" and ramp up their temper is where they would be well served. Leveraging that extra energy in other challenging endeavors could yield great results for those who are Weak. With proper mental training and focus, they could be very successful in careers related to sales. Also, for some, working on becoming more vulnerable in relationships would also serve them well.

Highlights of a Weak:

- Weak look anything but.
- They feel at home in a gym.
- They do well in careers where protection is Job #1 (think police officers, security detail, bodyguards, bouncers, personal trainers, etc.).
- They show others they care through personal protection.

Outward actions/appearances:

- Muscles, muscles, muscles; gym-rat type.
- Tends to be male oriented but not exclusively.

- Focus on fitness is not for wellness; it's mostly for physique and pure strength.
- Car choice tends to be big and masculine: SUV, Hummer, raised trucks.
- Showing off strength is the end in and of itself rather than being the means to an end like a Powerless.

Possible precipitating event:

Often are small in size for their age. May have been made fun of for being too skinny, too short, etc.

Small Target Issues:

- Constant focus on the next athletic achievement (e.g. lifting more weight, improving any metric associated with fitness).

Chapter Nine:
Dumb

Imbecilic, obtuse, stupefied, inane, insensate, unintelligent… in a word, dumb. The bigger the word, the better for those who are driven by a Dumb Human Operating System. Their vocabulary exceeds what most people consider to be normal. Dumbs enjoy illustrating their erudite vocabulary and take a lot of pride knowing and using words every day that most people don't know or haven't thought of since studying for their SATs or ACTs.

For those with a Dumb HOS, knowledge isn't a means to an end, it is the end. These people do not study to learn something that is always related to a direct purpose. They study for the acquisition of knowledge… and more and more and more knowledge. They crave it like a lion craves a juicy piece of meat. Their scholastic aptitude and how much they know is how they measure their success, and that is their complete source of pride.

The disconnect between knowledge for its own sake versus applicable knowledge is one of the very clear distinctions between Dumbs and Incompetents. The Dumbs are on a quest for knowledge. It's knowledge for knowledge's sake with them. Knowledge, in and of itself, intrigues and entertains Dumbs. On the other hand, an Incompetent will learn to gain a skill to avoid being or seeming inadequate or ineffectual. The Incompetent strives to be proficient at everything, so their pursuit of knowledge is to support that desire. The desire of the Dumb is to simply learn more facts, and they get enjoyment out of simply sharing that with others.

Let me share with you a story about Bob. He's a professor with quite of number of degrees and advanced degrees that reflect his long list of scholarly achievements. Bob is not at all shy about sharing this information. Quite the opposite. His quest for knowledge has created "alphabet soup" to include all of his degrees after his name. There is room for little else on his business card. It's no surprise that he has been well published, and every new published work grows unnecessarily longer because he is certain to include every publishing credit he ever had whether or not it bears any relevance to the current article or book. Bob takes a lot of pride in being published. It's his personal validation.

Bob was born with a natural ability to learn and retain knowledge. He was always intellectually ahead of other kids his age and had an above average IQ. Because of this natural intelligence, he became bored with friends and classmates. Rather than joining other children in games, Bob preferred to read. You might call him a book carnivore. Friends might bemoan a rainy day that kept them inside; Bob was equally happy to stay inside reading regardless of the weather. While friends would describe their favorite class as recess or lunch, Bob had trouble deciding if his favorite class was math, science, or history.

This disconnect with his peers can lead to a pronounced social awkwardness. Because he was bored with his friends and spent little time with them, Bob never really developed the social skills needed to maintain deep relationships. In grade school, he received kudos for being the smartest, so he became very focused on continuing to prove just how smart he was.

On the other hand, he found spending time with his parents' friends intriguing. Their knowledge and life experiences created an "equal" playing field on which he could engage with them. He was often acknowledged by various elders in his world for his intelligence. The time he spent with adults was far more rewarding to Bob than was spending time with kids his own age.

Relationship Challenges

While Bob excelled in relationships with those three and four times his age, he was not as successful with those his own age, especially when it came to relationships of a more personal nature. Romance was not always an area of proficiency.

Those with a Dumb operating system may have difficulty in relationships because they do not tend to focus on others. Their focus is commonly on themselves and how much they know. If you ask Bob's ex-wife about why their marriage failed, she'll take responsibility for her half of it. Not Bob. He doesn't see what he did wrong. Nothing bad that happens is his fault, but he'll be very quick to take credit for all the good things that occur whether or not he was even truly involved.

Because their own brain power is a huge source of comfort and companionship, Dumbs can be a somewhat self-centered group. When Bob had to give the eulogy at his uncle's funeral, everything he shared turned the spotlight back on himself. His uncle was not into fishing, yet Bob spent several minutes sharing a story about the time the two of them went on a fishing expedition (at Bob's suggestion) flush with several examples of his uncle's failure at the task compared to Bob's success. He shared how his uncle could never catch a fish, how Bob had to choose the proper bait for his uncle. And when they took their daily cache home, Bob had to be the one to successfully fillet the fish because Uncle Benny seemed to just chop up the fish, leaving little to cook. His speech only served to underscore how Bob knew everything rather than to pay tribute to the one person who always accepted Bob no matter how odd and awkward he was.

He extolled himself as borderline genius to his nieces and nephews. They considered him to be borderline crazy. He could bore them to death with facts about history, and to be polite, they would pretend to listen while they were mentally scheming their escape from the conversation… er, make that lecture. The gifts Bob bought for them were always age inappropriate. As teens, he continued to give gifts designed for much younger children. The response was a polite "thank you" and an eye roll that might have disconnected optic muscles once their backs were turned.

Dumbs Impact the World

Obviously, there are also many positive qualities of those with the Dumb HOS. They truly enjoy sharing their knowledge and curiosity with others. It is their curiosity and quest for knowledge that can lead to the immense amount of knowledge we need for innovation.

We can thank those with Dumb operating systems for the great research that is often done at the collegiate level. Again, they provide much of the knowledge that helps us advance our technologies and even our medical advancements. Our world would certainly not be where it is today without those with the Dumb HOS in it.

In a world where Facebook posts illustrating dogs jumping in a pool or the idiot who tried to jump off a football goal post, only to nail his chin on the way down captures the attention of the mass majority of the world, posts about the latest scientific evidence of water on the planet Mars and what that could possibly mean about the possibility of life on another planet go unnoticed. In this kind of social world, Dumbs can struggle to find their place. They have a wealth of knowledge and can oftentimes lose the interest of others on topics that are of little interest to those with whom they are speaking. Imagine discussing quantum physics for two hours... at a New Year's Eve party. Fascinating for those with an insatiable quest for knowledge, but most would prefer to watch a ball drop and dance the night away. Pay attention to the information a Dumb has to share and you can learn a lot.

Dumbs don't set themselves apart with the cars they drive. Whatever it may be, it will be a reflection of being smart. You might catch a Dumb driving a Prius or a car with really cool technology or a plain old beater. Cars typically don't matter much to those with a Dumb OS. To paint with a broad brush and be a bit stereotypical, technogeeks, professors, and engineers often go through life with Dumb operating systems. That's certainly not to imply that all of them fall into this category or have Bob's lack of social skills, but I believe it will help you better understand the Dumb HOS. However, if you ever need to know something, ask a Dumb. If they don't know the answer, they'll be happy to research it and figure it out for you… the perfect excuse to gain more knowledge. The downside is that you'll have to endure the full dissertation when they deliver the answer. No *Reader's Digest* version with them.

In terms of their finances, monetary success is not always important. It isn't that they can't make a lot of money or command high salaries. In fact, many of them have careers in high-paying fields. After all, they are commonly behind the scientific advancements that help keep humans alive. The thing about money is that it is simply not important to the Dumbs. It is not their yardstick for measurement against others or success. They value being recognized for what they know far more than for what they earn.

Unlike the Weak HOS that really tends to be male dominated, the Dumb HOS affects both men and women. It may skew more male, but not to the degree that the Weak HOS does. There are plenty of women who are fascinatingly smart but socially awkward and driven by the Dumb HOS. I used to live next to one. She was absolutely brilliant… she was an attorney who also had her pilot's license and even learned how to reverse engineer various chemicals and drugs. Many a college students would have loved her as a contact. She was an absolutely fascinating woman, but self admittedly, socially uninterested. She preferred spending time nurturing her 16 cats instead (I'm not exaggerating).

Whether it's men or women, Dumbs tend to remain single or go through multiple divorces. Some never leave the nest or return and stay. There are plenty of relationship challenges for Dumbs because of their inward focus. This can turn them so intensely inward that their spouses feel they lose any connection they had with them altogether. Like Bob, Dumbs tend to have a natural intellectual ability that creates boredom for them in social situations. Their fascination is in gaining knowledge that, in turn, gains them attention for what they know. That positive reinforcement sends them "back to the books" to gain more knowledge for another round of positive reinforcement. It becomes an unending cycle. If a Dumb happens to marry an Unlikeable, the marriage is almost doomed from the start. One may even question how they got married in the first place. The Unlikeable's need to constantly be socializing does not match up with the Dumb's need to remain at home. On the contrary, if two Dumbs match up, this could be a serious force to recon with. They may feed on each other's quest for knowledge and satisfy the need that each of them has for high intellectual stimulus.

Distinction: Dumbs vs. Incompetents

Dumbs have greater relationship challenges than those with Incompetent operating systems. The Incompetents have a much greater level of social awareness because it's important to them to be very competent... in everything... including their social dealings and relationships. Remember, Incompetents have to excel at everything. They may not rival their Dumb counterparts in intelligence, but they have the ability and desire to focus on and exceed at everything around them. Incompetents have a need for things to work – so they fix them if they get off track. The heads of those with a Dumb HOS may be so deep in books and/or computers that they don't even notice when their relationship is struggling before it is too late.

If you're familiar with the television show, *The Big Bang Theory*, think of Sheldon Cooper. A Dumb? Bet the house on it.

Highlights of a Dumb:

- Probably the smartest person you know.
- They feel at home in the world of academia.
- Generate much of our technological and medical advancements.
- Knowledge, research and reading – a short list of their favorite activities.
- Inward focus, if not appreciated and accepted, creates relationship obstacles.
- Constant need for intellectual stimulus.

Outward actions/appearances:

- Enjoy showing off vocabulary and intelligence.
- Knowledge isn't a means to an end (as with Incompetent); Dumbs gain knowledge only for the sake of more knowledge.
- Hold many advanced degrees and flaunt those.
- Socially awkward as they have trouble having two-way conversations.
- Cars will reflect latest technology or be a beater – the car itself is relatively unimportant.
- Monetary success is not a driver for them even though many Dumbs have careers in high-paying fields.

Possible precipitating event:

Innate ability to learn and retain knowledge can lead to boredom with less knowledgeable friends/peers.

Small Target Issues:

- Intense focus on gaining more knowledge and learning the next thing (e.g. continual pursuit of academic degrees).
- Teaching others about what they know (whether the listener is interested or not).

Dumb

Chapter Ten:
Outcast

It's all about FOMO with those who have an Outcast Human Operating System. What's FOMO? It is at the very core of those with this HOS: **F**ear **O**f **M**issing **O**ut. The Outcasts always, always, always have to be in the mix. Claustrophobia, agoraphobia, arachnophobia… you name the phobia, and for an Outcast, it will always place second behind their fear of not being part of the action, their fear of something happening without them.

While the Unlikeables may be the life of the party, the Outcasts simply have to be *at* the party. In addition to being at the party, they're usually also the last ones to leave, and very likely the first ones to arrive. They don't want to miss a thing. Sure, parties and events are fun, but for those with other Human Operating Systems, there's nothing wildly attractive about going out *all… of… the… time*. However, for the Outcasts, going out is their life and how they truly define themselves.

The Unlikeables are super-likeable people, and people gravitate toward them because they work hard to be very amicable and friendly. On the other hand, Outcasts may not be the most likeable people and at times can be downright off putting. It can be exhausting to hang out with an Outcast, especially if they're the one creating or coordinating the event.

If you'd ask those who know Carla to describe her, "professional socialite" would be the phrase used by nearly everyone. In Carla's mind, being part of the action and in the mix is her job, and it's one she takes seriously. She plans and coordinates many events; however, she makes sure to attend every single event she's invited to and even goes to those she hears about through the grapevine. Carla isn't shy about wrangling an invitation if she hasn't been invited. Her fear of missing out trumps any thought of being impolite about it.

Besides "professional socialite," you can add "military brat" behind Carla's name as well. Her family moved quite a bit from base to base, and Carla attended ten different schools in almost as many years. Granted, not all of those kids in military families develop the Outcast Human Operating System, but for Carla, the continual relocations as a youngster were the precipitating event for her to become an Outcast. After a while, moving away from friends became somewhat normal, but the first move or two were devastating to her. She couldn't imagine life without the best friend she had in kindergarten. In her young mind, she schemed endlessly about how the family could stay put to avoid losing her BFF. Neither her officer father nor Uncle Sam bought any of her ideas, and despite a flood of tears for days, Carla was uprooted. Once at her new school, she finally formed a new close friendship, but that also fell by the wayside with the next relocation. She fought about that move too, with no greater success than the first one. After that, Carla became adjusted to moving and losing friends. However, by this time, the Outcast hijacker had taken over control of her life.

You know those kids who fight going to bed? The ones who need another drink of water, another flimsy reason to leave their bedroom, the ones who do whatever it takes to stay awake because sleep brings with it the possibility of missing something… even if it's a group of boring adults talking about incredibly boring things. That was Carla. Other kids might just crash on the couch when they got too tired. Not Carla; she fought sleep at every turn if there were other people around. FOMO by age six. As an adult, she'll stay at the party until the wee hours no matter what time she may have to get up the next morning.

Carla doesn't particularly care for the symphony or the opera, but she has season tickets to both in her city because a group of friends loves to attend. Carla, with her Outcast hijacker in control, spends a lot of money on these performances that absolutely bore her to death. A non-Outcast person can quickly see the ridiculousness of spending money and time on something you dislike for no other reason than FOMO, but for Carla, there is no choice. For Carla, it makes her feel like she's part of the group… even though she socializes with this group of friends on other occasions that she enjoys more than the symphony and opera.

Outcast vs. Unlikeable

Carla's reaction to this is a bit typical for an Outcast. Unlikeable HOS folks don't have to attend *every* event, but an Outcast does… as long as it meets their standards. Carla associates the symphony and opera with high society, so she's quick to join in. Unlikeables don't necessarily have those same standards – nothing is below them and everyone's invited. This isn't true for the Outcast. The Outcast has greater social standards, and with those, it encourages a certain level of snobbishness.

With these standards, the Outcasts's social network can ebb and flow, and they may move between circles of friends, depending on who's on top socially. Conversely, Unlikeables continuously gather friends. For them, "the more, the merrier" no matter what anyone's social status may be. Greater numbers of friends drive validation for the Unlikeable. For the Outcast, they're more discerning about the social status of their friends, and the higher the level of that status, the more validated they feel.

A lot of people are uncomfortable with public speaking and rank it very high on their list of most feared activities. Not so with an Outcast. They are incredibly comfortable speaking to large groups and often seek out the opportunity. They want the spotlight and to be center stage as often as possible. Unlikeables can also show a proclivity for public speaking but usually not to the degree that Outcasts do.

Always One Better

One-upmanship plays a big role in the hijacked life of an Outcast. They may buy the same car as someone they admire, but they'll have to go one better. Maybe it's the same cool Jeep as a buddy, but it will have extra features, so they don't appear to be copying. As with finances, Outcasts have a tendency to "keep up with the Joneses" – a tendency that gets expensive and can be a huge derailer if the person truly does not have the income to support it. Spending habits speak to each HOS in different ways. Unlikeables spend money to treat and entertain their friends, being the ones to quickly pick up the tab and gain approval by doing so. Failures spend money to exhibit their success to others. The Outcasts will spend money to fit in and belong in the group. In essence, their purpose in spending money is to fit in at events. Having the right outfit to "fit in" or even just to attend the event can be expensive. Carla's tickets to the symphony and opera are the perfect example of this.

In their relationships, Outcasts face similar challenges to Unlikeables. Both have a tendency to always want to be on the go and in the mix. When one partner doesn't gravitate toward that pace or when they don't have the same desire to mix and mingle with a particular social set, relationship harmony can go awry. At the same time, an Outcast sees a competition in terms of fitting in with or living up to the spouse. The spouse doesn't necessary view it from that perspective, but the Outcast does. Again, relationships can falter if the spouse becomes extraordinarily successful, winning reward trips or going to top notch restaurants with clients and colleagues can make an Outcast feel "left out." That FOMO causes the hijacker to grip the steering wheel tighter and maintain control.

Highlights of an Outcast:

- The Fear of Missing Out is a key driver of behavior.
- Their social life is their highest priority.
- Socialites often fall into this type.
- They know what is going on at all times.
- They can over extend themselves financially by attending every event.

Outward actions/appearances:

- FOMO (fear of missing out) is the sole driver for an Outcast.
- Going out/being with other people is the focus of their lives.
- While Unlikeables tend to be friendly, an Outcast can be off putting as they'll wrangle their way into every situation... just to be in the situation.
- "Professional socialite" who may have snobbish standards.
- Exhibit "one-upmanship" and "keeping up with the Joneses" in car choices and other social situations.
- Outcasts spend money to fit in.

Possible precipitating event:

Possible precipitating event: moving from place to place as a young child. Never really feeling like they fit in.

Small Target Issues:

- Intense focus on fitting in and attending every event/party.
- Constant need to join the next club or organization.

Chapter Eleven:
Failure

Enviable success. Sometimes ostentatious. Conspicuous consumption. The best of everything. Get the picture? Then you're picturing someone with the Failure Human Operating System. They've made it in the world... and they like to show everyone who knows them that they've made it. There is no hesitation to spend a lot of money to illustrate their success. Buildings with their names on them (and possibly airplanes and helicopters as well). Appearances matter.

The Failures are typically people who have created a lot of successes in their world, and those successes are very career focused. Failures find themselves in fields where there is the possibility of great monetary success: financial advisors, entrepreneurs, real estate investors, lawyers, to name a few. Also, Failures seek professions with respect – think doctors, investment bankers and so on. Again, before we go any further, let me take a moment to reiterate that this is a tendency, and I am not suggesting that everyone who pursues a career in one of these fields is then operating with a Failure HOS. While it may be a stereotype, I believe it will help you understand this operating system. As with all of the HOS types, we all have one, and your ability to recognize yours is the first step in re-gaining control and sending your personal hijacker packing... or at least removing him from the driver's seat.

It is easy to confuse Failures with Incompetents. The reason is that Incompetents are also driven by success, but they're striving for "competence" in every facet of their lives – career, relationships, parenthood, etc. For the Failure, the success focus on career is much more of a laser beam. Failures also thrive when there is a competition. They may even create a competition where there is none. On the contrary, Incompetents and Unlikeables can be equally successful in their careers and in their finances, but they are not so inclined to make everyone aware of it. The hijacker in a Failure's life is driven to show it off.

Winning Is Everything

Eric has a Failure operating system. You notice him when he walks into the room: designer suit, expensive shoes, and jewelry – a lot of jewelry, a fancy watch. Like his father before him, Eric has made his money in real estate. Eric shares his father's name as well and is a "Jr." His family has been wealthy for as long as Eric can remember. His father was successful, but his father was also a very judgmental parent. Second best wasn't good enough – not for him… and certainly not for his kids. Having kids with low standards is not an option for Failures, so the pressure was on for Eric, especially being his father's only son.

The only way Eric could get his father's attention was by winning. Okay, let's correct that: The only way Eric could get positive attention from his father was by winning. Eric equated positive attention to his father's affection and love. Strike out in the t-ball game and endure an evening of being ignored or lectured. On the contrary, a home run meant a stop for ice cream and a lot of bragging on Eric's behalf.

At the young age of 28, Eric drives the biggest, fanciest BMW available, the 750i. It has all the bells and whistles. When those bells and whistles become commonplace features, it's clearly time to upgrade, regardless of the monthly payment or his actual ability to realistically cover it. His monthly car payment far exceeds what any accountant or financial planner would recommend, but Eric is unwilling to give that up. It makes a statement, and he will find a rational reason why he needs it. In his mind, his clients need to see that he is successful so that he is welcomed to their "club of wealth." He will not give up anything that doesn't support his desire to illustrate or validate his wealth. Remember, appearances matter for a Failure. Eric is all about illustrating his financial success with his car, house, clothing... everything, no matter the cost.

Sure, he makes a lot of money, but he also spends a lot, too. Financial planning, despite his background in real estate and a hefty income, is not necessarily his strength. His desire for the finer things trumps his desire to balance his checkbook. He prefers financial spending. He holds the belief that he can always make more money if needed.

There is no shortage of people with a Failure HOS in the world, and there are plenty of them in the U.S. These people are the self-promoters, and they do a great job at it. Whether or not their finances and priorities are as out of balance as Eric's, they spend – first and foremost – to illustrate their success. Eric's choice of vehicle is very typical for those with this HOS. An Incompetent won't drive a beater because it's important that he or she feels successful with their choice of a car. However, the distinction lies in how the car feels to them, personally on the inside. Does it feel good to be in the car and does it have great features making it a joy to drive. For the Failure, what's important is what the car looks like on the outside.

Failures derive their worth from their accomplishments and by their accomplishments. I'm talking about career accomplishments. The number of friends they have isn't nearly as important. The majority of their social relationships are only important to the extent to which those relationships help to underscore their career success. The status that their friends carry matters. Are they connected? Does their socio-economic status "qualify"? For the Failures, their whole world is defined by what they accomplished this year, this month, this week, or even today. Their success is envied by most and can often intimidate many peers and people their age unless they have a list of accomplishments themselves that can compare to that of the Failure.

The work ethic of a Failure can be revered. Working 80 hours a week is not out of the question if it means accomplishing the goal – being the best. Failures go the extra mile. They exude a tremendous amount of energy that the rest of us wish we could snag a small portion of. Very often, the salesmen at the very top of the chart are made of the cloth of a Failure. They are the most driven individuals in a profession. Some may even say psychotically so.

Failures are also some of the most trained in their respective professions. They hire coaches and trainers, attend seminars, and often become members of various clubs that include members who they can emulate.

Relationship Roller Coasters

The very trait that attracts a mate to a Failure can also be the source of their contention. That said, and as you can imagine, there can be plenty of relationship challenges in the life of the Failure. Their emotions can be a roller coaster depending on what may be happening in business that day. Close a sale and the world couldn't be better. Lose a negotiation or have it not go exactly their way, and it couldn't be more sour for them.

A top priority for this type is winning, and Failures are people who will run themselves into the ground, working exorbitant hours to achieve more. Yet, more is never enough. Their schedules create a great deal of stress for themselves and their families. Spouses and children may have trouble accepting their position on the priority list of a Failure. In the mind of a Failure, the value they provide their family is on making sure their family has the best of everything. It is not that their family isn't important – they are very much so– but time with them is often sacrificed in order to ensure they are providing the most they can for them. The intentions between a Failure and their family can be misconstrued. A Failure sees providing the best for his/her family as serving them as best he can. But often, what the family wants most is for their mom or dad to be home.

Their love is shown through extravagant vacations, living in the nicest home (or homes) and dressing them in the finest clothes and sending them to the best schools. Their love for their family isn't less than other operating systems, it is simply illustrated differently. It is helpful for the spouse of a Failure to understand its underpinnings. To recognize that the love for the family is not less than the next person, but it just shown by his ability to provide. The more hours spent at work is an investment into the family in the eyes of a Failure.

Additionally, Failures can be difficult to please since the precipitating incident for this HOS was their own inability to gain the approval and affection of an adult in their lives who mattered. Maybe it was a parent, teacher, or coach. The Failure may also see their spouse and children as additional illustrators of their own success. A Failure believes that the ultimate skill they can teach their child is "grit," work ethic, and drive. They don't believe in a trophy for everyone – you have to "deserve" it by earning it. With that said, they will be the first to stand up and celebrate their child's successes. This is an HOS that can be perpetuated from generation to generation, especially if both parents are Failures. For their children, it becomes all they know and seems normal.

Highlights of a Failure

- They are some of the most driven individuals.
- They enjoy winning.
- They believe in cultivating grit and work ethic.
- They illustrate their love by working hard and providing.
- They place a high value on continued education and training.
- They can be an emotional roller coaster – high after a win – low after an upset.
- They are the top earners and producers.

Outward actions/appearances:

- Want and display "the best of everything"; they're successful and they show that off in all facets of their lives.
- Career focused; derive self-worth from career accomplishments.
- Conspicuous consumption in wardrobe, jewelry, cars, etc.
- Appearances matter.
- Not necessarily good at managing finances despite wealth; focus is on spending.
- Winning is everything.

Possible precipitating event:

Possible precipitating event: inability to gain the approval and affection of an adult in their lives who mattered. Could have been that the main source of positive attention from a key adult figure was from accomplishment.

Small Target Issues:

- Making more and more and more money.
- They have a constant fear of losing it all.
- Energy spent on winning at all costs.

Failure

Chapter Twelve:
Bad

You try to do everything right. Please everyone. Follow the rules. Color inside the lines. If these statements are ringing a bell with you, striking close to home, you're under the influence of a Bad Human Operating System.

Katie is operating with a Bad HOS. She's the ultimate people pleaser. Everything she does is to please others. She works tirelessly to have the perfect house, perfect husband, perfect kids, perfect credit score, and perfect life, or at least to make all of those things look perfect. Nothing is ever out of order. She drives the speed limit and never thinks of cutting in front of anyone... ever. Katie always smiles, but to be perfectly honest, Katie is depressed much of the time.

There's a lot of stress that goes into constantly striving for her level of perfection, and let's face it, ongoing perfection is pretty much impossible. It's a self-perpetuating catch-22. The more perfect she makes things, the higher she perceives the bar to be. She can never reach it, let alone maintain it, but she can't let others know that, so the stress she puts herself under eats away at her – the perfect breeding ground for depression.

Growing up, Katie was always the teacher's pet. She was the poster child for the good little girl who never misbehaved and did everything right. The rules for everything were carved in stone in Katie's world. Katie's mother was one who could and did put the fear of God in her. If you ask Katie to recall a childhood incident in which she didn't follow the rules, she'll tell you about the time she uttered a curse word (one of the ones her father used regularly), and her mother had the proverbial cow over it. Grounded for a week. No television. No playground. Oh, and forget about attending the Brownie meeting that week. The punishment certainly didn't fit the crime. What it did do, however, was to let the Bad hijacker jump in and start driving Katie's life.

Ironically, the best friend, Annette, in the story where my hijacker was born, was indeed "Bad." Hence, it was why she was so diligent in practicing our dance choreography daily. She wasn't about to upset her mom who was so devoted to dance. On the plus side, it made her a better dancer. On the down side, it also made her a bit sad inside. Who doesn't want to just be accepted by their parents... of all people! Even while I type this, I recall getting into a "fight" with Annette was over an Emotion Cube. I wanted it on "Happy," and she insisted it should be on "Sad." Might have just been a momentary feeling, but it turns out that it may have been more telling about how her longer-term emotional state was as she suffered from anxiety and depression for much of her adult life.

I came across a poem that reminded me of someone with this HOS. I have not been able to locate its author, so for now it will be marked as "Anonymous":

Perfect Little Girl

Perfect little girl, who will always hide,

puts a smile on her face, keeps the pain deep inside,

No one to love her, no one to care,

No one to feel her pain, no one to share,

Perfect little girl, afraid to be free,

she's seen everything you wouldn't want to see,

She seems so happy but you'll never know,

that the smiles and the laughter are all one big show,

Perfect little girl, wants to get out,

reaches for the knife, though she's still filled with doubt,

her life has to end, she can't take it no more,

She can't go on pretending, why should she, what for?

Perfect little girl, she's made up her mind,

she's leaving her life, and the pain behind,

She no longer has to keep up her perfect little mask,

she's finally released, escaped herself at last,

Perfect little girl.... is perfect no more.

It's All about Behavior

The precipitating event for this HOS is much like the one that occurs for Failures: acceptance by an adult figure that the child holds in high regard. The distinction between the two is that for the Failure, they believe acceptance and love are based on the outcome. For the Bad, they believe acceptance and love is derived from the behavior, regardless of the end result. Both seek and relish acceptance from the alpha adult in their world, but the behavior of the Failure is less important as long as positive results occur. For the Bad, it's all about the behavior. It doesn't matter so much if you lose, but you'd better be darn certain to play by the rules.

The Bad HOS represents a bit of a gender bias. While it could go either way, it leans more female. There is a certain expectation that little boys will misbehave. The old "boys will be boys" adage. However, when girls misbehave, there's a disconnect and more judgment about behavior. "Sugar and spice and everything nice, that's what little girls are made of." Since Human Operating Systems are created at a young age, with this typical bias between boys and girls, it's not surprising that the Bad HOS is more prevalent in women.

While those with a Failure HOS have a certain career niche (fields in which there is the possibility for great monetary reward), the same is not necessarily true for Bads. There is nothing defining about their career choice; they're simply looking to do the right thing, however they define it. They will be diligent in their work day, following policies to the letter and never failing to meet deadlines. Their "i's will always be dotted and t's crossed."

Bads are often very good with money, no matter how much they may earn. Saving is the right thing to do, so they do it. They have very good credit scores because they pay their bills on time (so long as they are able to). That's what you're supposed to do. A late payment, if it occurs, is a huge stressor! Regardless of spirituality, I have seen a lot of Bads in my coaching work as regular church goers. As we peel back the onion in sessions, it becomes apparent that church attendance occurs because it's the right thing to do and is not always founded in true, personal spirituality.

The motto of the Bad is: avoid confrontation at all costs. Confrontation is not following the rules in the Bad's mind. In relationships, this becomes problematic. Bads can easily be taken advantage of because they rarely, if ever, stand up for themselves. That would be confrontational, and confrontation breaks the rules. To an extreme degree, women with a Bad HOS can find themselves in abusive relationships. Their hijacker supports being taken advantage of to the point of accepting abuse. Yes, that is an extreme instance, but sadly, it's accurate. And because they have become proficient at putting their best face forward – always a smile – often the abuse can go unnoticed, for they don't typically complain about their spouse.

As people pleasers, the Bads very often compromise a bit of themselves. They will do and agree to things that run counter to their values because they want to please others. Disagreeing or being confrontational is not pleasing behavior, and pleasing others is paramount. As you can easily imagine, this drives a great deal of anxiety. These people also tend to have a lot of skeletons in the closet. Honestly, we have all done things that we shouldn't have. A Bad will work so hard to keep the things they've done "wrong" hidden. They will never discuss these things. This is also a huge stressor because it can eat away at them inside.

The Bad HOS can easily be mistaken for Unlovable. They both tend to be high people pleasers. The major distinction lies more in their behavior. Always following the rules, doing what they are supposed to be doing as seen by their superiors. Unlovables, while it can be difficult, can speak up for themselves when pushed. On the other hand, someone with a Bad HOS goes internal, beating themselves up rather than standing up for themselves, which is a major source of suffering.

The Survival Mechanism at Work

As I mentioned at the beginning, the hijacker is a survivalist and will work incessantly to continually prove that, in the case of this HOS, the person is, in fact, bad. That was the vicious circle in which Katie found herself. In high school, just when she had proven to teachers and staff that she was the "good girl," she got caught doing "naughty" things with her boyfriend at school (in a parochial school, no less) – the boyfriend her parents knew nothing about. She wanted to please him, despite it being against the rules. Just as her hijacker was getting comfortable, feeling like it was in control – keeping Katie in line – her HOS had to fight harder to protect its identity and validate that she is, in fact, Bad.

Highlights of a Bad:

- They are rule followers – they follow the rules everyone else creates.
- They avoid confrontation.
- They occur as very happy people who have their lives perfectly put together.
- Their suffering is often below the surface. They would rather talk to you about you, so they do not reveal any difficulties (or to them imperfections) they face.
- When the Bad hijacker is well managed, these people make great employees because they are diligent in their work.
- This type is another type that greatly compromises self for the sake of others.

- This type can be most often confused with Unlovable.

Outward actions/appearances:

- Ultimate people pleaser.
- Perfect house, spouse, kids, and credit.
- Teacher's pet.
- Avoids confrontation at all costs.
- Tends to be female oriented but not exclusively.
- Always plays by the rules.
- Very good with money because saving and paying bills on time constitutes playing by the rules and doing the right thing.

Possible precipitating event:

Possible precipitating event: childhood incident in which the Bad didn't follow the rules and experienced a punishment that far exceeded the crime; acceptance and love is derived from being on their best behavior.

Small Target Issues:

- Constant focus on making things perfect; whatever is perceived as out of alignment is the next focal point to make it perfect.
- Energy spent on following the rules with focus on behavior not outcome.

Bad

Chapter Thirteen:
Recognizing Your Own Human Operating System

Now that we've covered the various Human Operating Systems as I've outlined and defined them to date, the next step may be an uncomfortable one: It's time to recognize your own HOS. Before you are too quick to think about many of the negative or less attractive traits that were revealed as we covered each of the operating systems and wave them all off, believing that none of those applies to you (or that you have some of every single one, so no one HOS truly defines you), let me take a minute to remind you of what a Human Operating System really is.

Like computers, we *all* have operating systems working behind the scenes. Without the operating system in a computer, all of the helpful, supportive, and cool apps and software that are available are entirely useless. Also like a computer, sometimes the Human Operating System needs a tune up or a full re-boot. If you are anything like me, I don't consider rebooting my computer or smartphone until it starts to get quirky or not operate effectively and ignore the fact that rebooting on a regular basis is healthy for the effective operation of my devices. Cleaning up and refreshing the system can help prevent the dreaded system crash. Perhaps you've had some sort of crash in your life – a failed relationship, a job loss, or business fiasco. Or perhaps it's not something quite so catastrophic that is causing you to re-evaluate what is happening in your life, but rather a certain sluggishness – thinking that things are not humming along like they did before that brought you into the pages of this book.

You're open-minded enough to realize that there are repeated patterns in your life that are causing problems and limiting your success and happiness; however, you are unable to truly understand them... let alone break those patterns. You have goals and aspirations for your life that continue to be out of reach. Or, like some, you reach certain goals driven by your HOS, only to sabotage others (e.g., sabotaging relationships because you are so driven to succeed in your career). Perhaps your fingers brush against them but can't quite grab them. Maybe you want to attain a lofty goal that seems wildly out of reach.

As I told you at the beginning of this book, repeated patterns that garner negative results are caused by the hijacker that took over control of your life, and you actually lost that control at a young, impressionable age. You lost control during a precipitating incident that created your Human Operating System at around age four to six... no matter how irrelevant that incident or situation may seem now as you recall it from your adult perspective many years or decades later. I repeat this because it is important to recognize that the voice inside your head that drives you in a certain, default direction is the actual voice of an approximate 5-year-old and not the conscious voice of the intelligent adult you have become. The same voice you talk back to as you try to convince yourself how silly it is to be intimidated by a wealthier person, a more social person, or a more attractive person.

Think about that for a moment... even as I type them, these words literally sound like they came straight out of the mouths of kids in elementary school. And yet, as adults, we still have these insidious, insecure thoughts that hold us back from opportunities. They hold us back from truly having a life and business by our ultimate design.

Also remember that while a computer operating system works to balance resources (more RAM here, less RAM there, so programs and apps work as efficiently as possible and making the most of battery life), the Human Operating System is not *at all* proficient in this task. In fact, the HOS and the hijacker in your life will almost always direct all resources toward a single goal: *self-preservation of an existing identity – a known and familiar identity.* Think of it as a tug-o-war between the identity created by a 5-year-old and the adult you have become as a result of that internal voice. This is why it gets confusing. The people who know you and interact with you see a bit of a different person than your hijacker does.

Critical Distinction

Trying to distinguish between an insecurity and a Human Operating System can be challenging; however, there is a clear difference. While the HOS is a *form* of an insecurity, the HOS actually becomes a part of your personal identity and the difference lies in its outward manifestation. For example, if you are socially insecure, you tend to exude that constantly. You are shy and tend to stay in the background. People recognize your insecurity and will even describe it as: "She's very quiet and tends to be a wall flower at parties." For the insecurity, it is what it appears to be. On the other hand, the Human Operating System manifests itself as the exact opposite. Someone with an Unlikeable HOS is the life of the party. The guy with the Dumb HOS is eloquent and extremely intelligent.

It's important to keep this critical distinction in mind as you work through the following exercises to recognize and define your own HOS. I have a lot of coaching clients who mistake an insecurity for their HOS. A simple insecurity shows up as an insecurity. An HOS will stump those around you because you simply *do not* resemble your Human Operating System at all. You occur as the exact opposite of your HOS. That is the distinction. The insecure feelings that your HOS conjures up are *ONLY* experienced inside your head. There is no outward evidence of it seen by others.

For example, if you are insecure socially, you will still be noticeably shy. You may only speak to those you know in a room full of people, rather than approach strangers and introduce yourself. If you had the Human Operating System of Unlikeable, you would occur very differently in that same room full of people. Instead you would be the one navigating the room, learning the names and about the lives of a great number of people before you leave for the evening, all the while evaluating – inside your head – the instance or instances that you question if you made someone feel comfortable or doubting something you said to someone.

If you are insecure about your appearance, you may not spend thousands of dollars on outfits despite this feeling as it is not a priority for you. But if your HOS is Ugly, much of your resources (time and money) would be dedicated to ensuring that you never left the house without being completely put together.

If you are insecure about being in front of an audience of people, your Human Operating System is not likely to be Powerless because Powerless types love being in that position. They thrive on it. Instead, Powerless would do what they could to make sure they had a spot on the speaking agenda.

In each of these examples, you will notice that an insecurity is an insecurity. It appears just as it feels. We typically don't spend a lot of time and money "working on" that insecurity. Whereas, an HOS doesn't resemble an insecurity at all to the outside world – even though you may have insecure thoughts about it that resemble an insecurity. The bottom line is that other people can notice your insecurities, but they are blinded to your Human Operating System because you occur to them as "having that handled."

It's possible that you were able to immediately recognize your HOS as you read through each of the descriptions and examples. You may have read a phrase or two and thought, "Yup, that's me." Or you were able to fully empathize with the person whose story you read... and saw many similarities between that person and yourself. It's also possible that you had a strong emotional response of *NOT* wanting to be *THAT*! (This could be another clue). Maybe you are still trying to recognize and define your HOS. No matter which of those situations (immediate recognition or undecided) describes you at this point, the exercises that follow will help you recognize your true HOS.

In order to achieve the life you want, one by design, you must be able to manage your HOS, and in order to manage it, you must first recognize it! Failing to do so will render you vulnerable to a life by default. A life unintended, unfulfilling, full of frustration or simply "lackluster." This is not to sound to grave. Many people feel pretty satisfied with their lives and just feel that there is a missing piece… as in the example I gave about the highly successful business owner who just can't seem to hold down a fulfilling relationship with someone special to share in that success or the highly social person with a thousand friends who feels that they never really get their own needs met because they are too "self-sacrificing" or too focused on others to meet their own needs.

More often than not, there is one particular area that continues to be a source of frustration. And that is the reason this topic is so important – balance or the overall design can only be achieved when you become familiar with your HOS and learn how to use it to benefit you.

Exercise #1

The HOS is the major "default" design element in humanity. It generates your response to every situation. It's in charge and working to keep it that way. However, when you are aware of it, that awareness gives you the opportunity to consciously redesign and redirect your responses.

Let's take a moment to review the major HOS types:

- Unlovable
- Powerless
- Incompetent
- Ugly

- Unlikeable
- Weak
- Dumb
- Outcast
- Failure
- Bad

It's probably helpful to think about the examples I presented for each of these and try to recognize the HOS of someone else first. I find that people can always peg the HOS of their spouse but often struggle to identify their own. That said, think about your spouse or someone else you know very well (maybe a close friend, your boss, a subordinate, a sibling, etc.) and think about the various traits exhibited consistently and to extremes in that person.

You will need to keep in mind that the traits you see have a direct opposite correlation to the Human Operating System. For example, a robust social life equals Unlikeable. An insanely driven and immensely successful person could equal Powerless or Failure. You can do the same thing with celebrities and politicians. Outward appearances and actions speak volumes about an HOS. I have summarized a few highlights for each of the Human Operating Systems below to help you decipher them.

For the Unlovable, there is a lot of nurturing and caring. This person has very deep relationships with others, but they can be roller coasters. Recall that Jasmine loved people entirely until she felt wronged by them. Then she threw them away. She was a very sweet person but had trouble maintaining relationships when she felt those relationships were "unequal." For her, the survival mechanism that often kicks in is that she will blow up a good, loving relationship over a seemingly innocuous thing. That is how her hijacker retains control.

For the Powerless, there is continual striving to reach the top. Aspirations for higher and higher positions of power. John gravitated toward contact sports and continued to be physically fit into his adult life. He has worked tirelessly to become the CEO, perhaps the youngest in the company's history. He's competitive on all fronts. It's difficult to become or stay better than John. He's all about being on top.

For the Incompetent, they're good (if not great!) at everything they do. They seem to have the Midas touch and are always right… or they think they're always right. Unlike the Powerless, they're not interested in climbing to the top, to be at the helm. Instead they are interested in being the best at whatever it is they're doing. I'm an Incompetent and saw success not as power but as tangible proof that I was not, after all, incompetent.

For the Ugly, they don't leave the house unless every detail of their outward appearance is perfect. Naomi was always color coordinated (outfit, shoes, purse, jewelry, nails), yet she was beautiful without the trappings. Naomi's closet is huge and its content is continuously updated. Time spent getting ready is never time wasted in Naomi's book.

For the Unlikeable, it's all about the party! Tons of friends on Facebook, connections on LinkedIn, and followers on Twitter. Check the contacts in your phone (or your "Unlikeable" friend's phone). Typically, the average person has 152 contacts (yes – there have been studies done on this). It wouldn't be surprising for an Unlikeable to have 600 contacts! Randy is always the life of the party and the center of attention. He thrives on being a connector and takes pride in creating success for others. Public speaking? Randy lives for it. People gravitate toward him, and he makes them laugh.

For the Weak, think about Charles Atlas. Plenty of muscles and living at the gym. Zack focuses on his body, working out, taking supplements that help him build himself physically. His time is spent on physical development much more than an on any other form of personal or professional development.

For the Dumb, there is no shortage of degrees listed behind his or her name. Vocabulary is extraordinary and the grade point average is off the charts. Henry has a long list of scholarly achievements and never fails to discuss them. His focus on academics leads to his social awkwardness and conversations that others may find boring, but he doesn't seem to notice. Often times, the conversation with a Dumb HOS is difficult for those of us with average intelligence to follow (or care to follow) Henry's driven to prove how smart he is and to be the ultimate fact checker.

For the Outcast, FOMO (fear of missing out) is a huge motivator. Carla doesn't have to be the life of the party; she simply has to be at the party. She participates in activities she doesn't particularly like because to miss them would be catastrophic. Going out is her life and she wouldn't have it any other way. She needs to be relevant in the social society in her metropolitan city. Socialites often fall into this HOS.

For the Failure, it's one successful venture after another, and they're striving to have the best of everything.

For Eric, appearances matter. While Incompetents are driven to be successful because of how it makes them feel about themselves and Powerless are driven to lead others and be at the helm, Failures are driven to success because of what they can have and how it makes them appear to others. Fancy cars, fancy house in a fancy neighborhood. Striving to have it all and to show it all.

For the Bad, people pleasing is high on the list. Katie does everything right and follows all the rules. She has the perfect spouse, perfect house, perfect kids, and even a perfect credit score. For Katie, perfection is always the goal, and the more perfection she attains, the harder it becomes to achieve and maintain it. Katie smiles all the time, and her teeth are perfect.

With that quick refresher of the HOS types, make a point to notice the HOS of those with whom you interact tomorrow and over the coming week. Notice what people wear, what they drive, and how they interact with others. Remember that HOS lives in the realm of opposites and is, in fact, often an over compensation of a self-perceived failure of the individual. Also, keep in mind that it is not a single clue that will point to someone's HOS, but the whole picture: their car, their house or neighborhood, their profession, their social lists and status, and so on.

Next, I want you to think of the five people who know you best. Write their names on a sheet of paper, and think about how they would positively describe you. Jot down the descriptive words that each would use. (If you'd like, you can actually ask them, but I find that asking typically isn't necessary as you will pretty much know what they'll say.)

The key here is that all five of the people you select would have to agree on three positive descriptors of you. For example, of five people describing me, they would all agree on the words: intelligent, poised and capable of a lot of things. This combination describes someone who is highly competent. The words nurturing, selfless, and always looking out for others point directly to an Unlovable. Well-spoken, well-read, and educated point to Dumb. The name of the HOS is always the opposite of what you think it would be. It is what your hijacker is working to cover up about you and has been for many years.

You'll find that the three positive descriptors overwhelmingly point to who you really are... and the opposite of that is your own HOS. In looking over the list and thinking about what might resonate with you, it's very important to keep in mind the distinction between an insecurity and an HOS. The HOS will always manifest as the opposite of outward appearance; an insecurity will not. An insecurity is still an insecurity. A Human Operating System is actually a proficiency.

Exercise #2

In Exercise Two, we're going to really turn the focus inward and on yourself. Previously, I asked you to start understanding Human Operating Systems by looking at others' outward appearances and actions to identify their HOS types. No doubt you've started pegging others with reasonable accuracy, and that was good practice to define your own HOS.

What is your "social mask"? Many times, we feel like we're putting up a pretense. I often hear people say that they feel like a "fraud." Others probably don't recognize it, except for those who are already adept at understanding the HOS concept. For example, those who know an Unlikeable would never use the word "unlikeable" to describe him. They're seeing the social mask, not the insecurities that created the social mask. However, in being entirely honest, the Unlikeable who has a been versed and has identified his own HOS will admit that even though he has developed great sociability, he continues to feel a bit of an internal discomfort that includes his fear of being Unlikeable. This simply serves to be a continual motivator to maintain his proficiency.

To help you dig deeper, answer these questions honestly about yourself. Keep in mind these answers are just for you; no one else needs to see them, so don't edit yourself and don't sugar coat your responses:

Profession:
Why did you choose your profession?

Does it reflect your aptitude or attitude? (e.g., those who are in social services tend to be very nurturing individuals; those in management tend to want to be in charge, etc.)

What are you most proud of in what you have accomplished? (You can list more than one – but please don't say "your kids" – for this exercise, they don't count.)

How does your profession make you feel about you?

What do you think your profession says about you?

Does it describe the successful side of you; the nurturing side; the powerful or dominant side?

What do you want your profession to project about you? When meeting someone new, think about how you describe your professional life to them. Do you accentuate your profession or minimize it?

How does your spouse describe you in your profession? S/he is best at...

Keeping in mind the various HOS types and in thinking about the stories of others that you've read, what is your profession compensating for?

Outward Appearances:

Look at how you typically dress: What does how you look say to the world?

Do you refuse to leave the house without being perfect or do you need someone to remind you to comb your hair?

Do you live for comfort or for style?

Are you fastidious or disheveled?

Are you fixed up and ready in 10 minutes or does it take you 90 minutes?

Do you dress for comfort or for style?

Do you wear name brands?

Look at your watch... or your jewelry. What does it tell others? What do you want it to say about you?

> Big, flashy and hard to miss? Or simplistic? Elegant? Non-existent? Sporty? Classy? Coordinated or one piece fits all events and outfits? Form or function?

What kind of car do you drive?

> As you'll recall, in the HOS examples, I always touched on cars because, like other outward appearances, cars are typically well thought out purchases and do say a lot about someone's HOS.

How do you handle your finances?

> What concerns do you have about money? Do financial concerns keep you up at night? Or is money merely a means to the end you desire?

> What is your credit score? Do you even know your credit score?

> Are you a saver or spender?

> What do you find you spend the most amount of money on? What do you enjoy shopping for?

What about your social calendar?

> Is it empty except for an annual holiday party and a few doctor appointments? Or so full of activities that you'll be juggling events in order to attend all of them?

> What is your "friend" count on Facebook? How does that compare to most of your friends' numbers? If not on Facebook, how many connections do you have on LinkedIn?

What does your ideal night consist of?

Think very honestly about your answers to these questions. In your answers, you'll discover what it is about yourself that you do not want the world to know. In my own situation, I didn't want the world to know I was incompetent. Remember my precipitating incident? Failing to be picked for the solo in a dance recital. Insignificant at this point? Absolutely! Yet that's what started the ball rolling for me, and through much of my early adult life, I realize now that everything I did was driven to hide from the world my self-perceived incompetence. Key phrase being "self-perceived." Once I have learned to recognize and manage my own HOS, I have grown quite fond of it. Because without it, I wouldn't have created the life and success I have today. (Nor would I have written this book).

If you could boil down what you are trying to hide from the world into one word, what would it be?

A good measure of arriving at your HOS type is that you cringe (at least slightly) when you say that word in relation to yourself. Does thinking of yourself as Powerless make you cringe? How about Unlovable? Dumb?

If you need to, read over the list of HOS types again and think about each one in relationship to yourself. Start by checking off all of the ones that it might be. If the "I am not" echoes loudly in your head when you reach a particular word, it's a good sign that you have hit on your own HOS. It will make you say, "I'm not that," and you'll begin thinking about all of your evidence to the contrary. Think about a Dumb type with multiple degrees to prove that he or she is not dumb. Or an Ugly with a wardrobe that supports the opposite. And don't try to minimize the word either. Be real with yourself:

- It's not "unintelligent." It's Dumb.
- It's not "unpopular." It's Unlikeable.
- It's not "unsuccessful." It's Failure.
- It's not "unattractive." It's Ugly.

You get the picture. Trying to sugar coat it makes you cringe about it less, and that's exactly what you don't want to do. The point of the exercise (and the book, for that matter!) is to recognize and admit your HOS. The more it makes you cringe, the more you have honed in on your HOS. Uncomfortable? Yes. But necessary in order for you to learn to manage it and kick your hijacker out of the driver's seat. Without being real with yourself and admitting to yourself what your HOS is, you won't be able to start altering your behavior and reactions to get what you want out of your life.

Once you have whittled the list down to a few, begin to ask yourself if you *are* each one. For example, someone who is painfully shy, may think their HOS is Unlikeable, but it's not. It is just another run of the mill insecurity. You want to identify the one that you have actually become very proficient at: If you are extremely well-read, straight-A student who has a couple of degrees to back you up, you are more likely to have a Dumb HOS (with an insecurity of being Unlikeable).

Exercise #3

Because your hijacker is a vital element of your identity – it's all about its own self-preservation and hiding itself from the world – without it, your identity is in jeopardy. It has very likely held you back in one or more facets of your life. The challenges, missed opportunities or unintended directions happen to the best of us with the best of intentions as a result of being unconscious (or unaware) of our Human Operating Systems. Misguided attention can have repercussions, both large and small. At best, they cause daily distractions. At their worst, they lead to completely misguided directions.

The focus on preparation can be another problematic area for Incompetents and Dumbs as they over-research everything before taking action, and that time spent could cause them to miss the proverbial boat on an opportunity. Perhaps in striving for perfection, they sacrifice the whole venture due to missing a deadline or scrapping an otherwise perfectly successful (or at least acceptable) project because it doesn't meet their standards. I have encountered countless Powerless types who have built successful financial practices to jeopardize them for the opportunity to be in leadership positions – only to later regret it. Don't get me wrong – leadership positions are often ideal for those with a Powerless HOS, but not *all* Powerless need to be at the top of the leadership pyramid.

Likewise, Bad Katie is missing out on her ability to enjoy her family and friends because she is too wrapped up in trying to achieve and maintain perfection. She's hiding a ton of stress behind her perfect smile, and in reality, it's eroding the happiness and enjoyment she should be getting out of life. She is under an illusion that her family and friends will only respect her if she has her life in perfect order all the time. In reality, they hardly notice if something is out of place or imperfect. But they may miss out on being able to spend meaningful time with her when her mind is on perfection.

Unlovables are sacrificing themselves to please others. Perhaps you didn't return to college because you felt you needed to support your spouse, giving up what you wanted for the benefit of someone else.

Similarly, Unlikeables do things that compromise themselves in order to fit in and gain friends. In some instances, this has been as extreme as drug use in order to feel like they fit in. An Outcast will have similar actions because being a part of the group is critical to them. Carla attended events she disliked simply because of her fear of missing out. That time would have been better spent on activities she enjoyed!

If you're a Dumb or Incompetent, you may refuse to take on a new hobby because you would not be good at it if you could not master it immediately. The need to be right is a common "shortcoming" for an Incompetent or Dumb. Try to live with someone who constantly argues their point even if it bears no consequence. It can erode relationships.

An example I often share is one that nearly happened to me as a result of my HOS. In my early twenties, I was on a mission. A mission to complete a master's degree at the top of my class (check), a mission to earn a very good income doing work I found fulfilling (check), and a mission to complete my PhD from UC Santa Barbara (Incomplete). At a point in my early twenties, I nearly unconsciously derailed an idyllic life I had already created as a leading coach in an up-and-coming field that would later explode into a full-fledged industry (business coaching). I say I *nearly* derailed it because had I allowed my hijacker to have her way, I would have given up my opportunity at the company I had just been hired into simply to complete a PhD in a field that would have garnered me a tremendous amount of respect but almost inevitably would not have been nearly as fulfilling or one that would have allowed me to create the life and business design that is ideal for me. The only purpose it would have served would have been one more validation to an insatiable need to prove that I was not, indeed, incompetent. In fact, I would have uprooted my life for it and given up doing what I already found as my perfect career and loved doing had I not recognized the potential pitfall. Looking back, I'm very grateful that I understood the impact of my HOS and managed it effectively which helped me avoid "missing my path." My goal is to help you do the same in your own life.

Exercise:

So what examples can you give for situations and decisions in which your own HOS held you back? Where has it blocked your ability to enjoy your life and achieve what you truly want? As with Exercise Two, you need to be honest about your answer. What's done is done, so being dishonest about or minimizing your answer does nothing to change it. Your ability to cite accurate, if uncomfortable or even painful, examples will help you solidify your HOS recognition. Was it a failed relationship? A missed opportunity? Lost experiences with your kids or loved ones? Or simply an overall lack of enjoyment? If you can't recognize it, you can't manage it. If you can't manage it, you can't take the necessary actions to avoid future missed opportunities that occur because your hijacker is in control.

Exercise #4

Take a deep breath, it's not all bad! While several of the examples and stories I've shared with you focus on many negative aspects and traits of the different HOS types, there is good news. Your HOS can also benefit and serve you… and probably has to this point in your life on some occasions.

In reading the HOS descriptions and stories of those with the various Human Operating Systems, you'll recall that I pointed out scenarios in which a particular HOS benefitted the person. For example, an Unlikeable is very well-suited for a successful career in sales. In Randy's case, he was able to land a lucrative sales position with an exclusive car manufacturer. He met the owner of one dealership as a result of networking with a client, and that subsequently put him in touch with the national manager who flew him to Europe, all expenses paid (and first class, to boot!) to visit the manufacturing plant. His ability to get the job and be successful with it was completely the result of his HOS.

In much the same way, the Powerless and the Failure no doubt can point to their respective operating systems as the foundation of their successes – gaining the corner office and the successful business ventures certainly aren't bad things. The Unlovable and the Outcast both have aspects of their relationships with others that are very beneficial and add to their lives. The Ugly may leverage wardrobe and looks to an advantage, or their uncanny ability to arrange the most perfect details of an event to create lasting memories for all those who attend it. The Weak may have an enviable track record in physical competition and if they are mindful about staying healthy, a great life of longevity without the traditional ailments that may cripple others. The Incompetents and Dumbs can use what they know to advance their careers, and a Bad probably doesn't have to worry about having saved enough for retirement.

With those examples in mind, think about how your HOS has advanced your career or otherwise made a positive impact in your life? I'm certain you will not have a problem being honest about your answer in this exercise.

Though much of this can sound doom and gloom, there is actually more good that can result from an HOS than bad, so long as you learn to manage yours. The lynchpin is your ability to first recognize your own HOS, so you will be able to better leverage the good without compromising and encountering the bad. When we become aware of our HOS, it allows us the option of choice. I'll even dare to say "free will." Your ability to choose – your free will – defines you as a human being. Left in the dark about what your HOS is, or even that you have one, makes "free will" a near impossibility. However, once you are aware of your Human Operating System and how to leverage it and be conscious about your choice, a whole world of your design becomes a real option. This consciousness and awareness allows you the control you need to design your life. It turns off the autopilot and moves your hijacker out of the driver's seat.

This recognition of your HOS is the critical first step in managing it. I hope that having gone through these four exercises, you now have a firm grasp on the Human Operating System that drives you. Perhaps you have even tried to recall what may have happened to you at a young age that created it. Maybe that incident is forever burned into your memory. It may take you a bit to recall this event, but when you hit on it, you will be able to recall it with tremendous clarity. It has created your HOS and you will never be rid of it, but you will learn to manage it and come to appreciate it. As you will soon learn, you don't *want* to be rid of it. It has served you, and served you well in most instances. The next step is learning how to manage it, and how to re-program it to be your advantage rather than your liability, holding you back.

My aim is to teach you how to leverage your Human Operating System to create more rewarding relationships, a more successful business and a more enriching life.

Chapter Fourteen:
Why Do We Self-Sabotage?

By definition, sabotage means to deliberately destroy, damage, or obstruct something for an advantage. The point of sabotage is to weaken the enemy. Wartime advantage is often gained through acts of sabotage, and the most effective saboteurs are often not an obvious, visible enemy. They are secret agents, underground operatives, double crossers, spies. Saboteurs work hard to conceal their identities, so they can carry out their directives for the outcomes *they* want.

Besides during wartime, there are examples of sabotage in industry (labor unions using it to gain negotiating advantage), in environmental actions (groups destroying property to obstruct development and construction), and certainly in politics (smear campaigns and similar actions to derail an election). While all of those can range from corrupt to downright unscrupulous, the worst sabotage is the kind that happens between your ears – self-sabotage.

Think about some of the key words in the sabotage definition: "deliberately" and "weaken the enemy." It's hard to imagine that anyone would work to deliberately weaken themselves, and who thinks of themselves as an enemy in the first place? We all do. Well, maybe not *us*, but the hijacker in each of our lives certainly does.

You've probably heard the phrases "I'm my own worst enemy," or "I can't seem to get out of my own way." Very likely, you've uttered those phrases at one time or another. I'm here to tell you that these are the phrases we use to explain the unconscious undercurrent that leads to our failures. When speaking in front of an audience, I like to uncover what the participants feel get in their way, "What's the number one thing that gets in the way of your business success?" Almost always, someone will shout out "I am." They recognize that it's himself or herself, but they can't seem to correct or at least stop their sabotaging actions. In essence, they can't get out of their own way. They truly are their own worst enemy.

In some explanations of self-sabotaging behaviors, it's defined as a conflict in your personality: one side of you wants one thing and the other side wants something different. The other side is your hijacker who is always in full survival mode. Your hijacker never wants to give up the driver's seat and relinquish control. Your hijacker is the double-crossing, underground operative, secret agent who is sabotaging you at every turn for his advantage and to get what he wants. Sabotaging you is your hijacker's survival mechanism.

It has been said, "to control thyself, know thyself." It is impossible to control what you do not know. The point of the exercises this book includes is to help you "know thyself" so that you can then "control thyself." So be sure not to skip through them.

Unconscious Reactions

You can probably list and enumerate times in your life when you did something self-sabotaging. And just as likely, you're confused about why you did it, what to do about it and how to correct this seeming need to self-sabotage. Nobody sets out to do this, but it happens daily. I'm certain you've never turned off the alarm, gotten out of bed, stood up, and said, "Today's the day. Today's the day I will sabotage myself! Today's the day I'm going to ruin my own chance to get what I really want." Yet it happens continually.

There are plenty of self-sabotaging behaviors, some of which can actually be life threatening. Consider the person who's overweight, whose doctor has warned them repeatedly that their health and, in fact, their very life depends on losing weight, yet they'll stuff themselves at the all-you-can-eat buffet and will choose to watch the next episode of their favorite show (or binge watch an entire season!) rather than going for a walk or going to the gym. Clearly, this person can't get out of their own way.

Or think about the person who's struggling to pay the bills and has the foreclosure notice on the top of the stack of bills, but he can't figure out how to stop frivolous spending on toys – the latest tech gadget, accessory, or the big shopping trip to Costco buying all the stuff he doesn't need… in bulk! He's in dire straits and is faced with losing his home, but he can't figure out how to stop and will justify his actions and behaviors the whole way along… right to the poor house. He's his own worst enemy.

In addition to those two examples, other self-sabotaging behaviors include fear of success or change, analysis paralysis bogging down in too many options, procrastination, quitting when the going gets tough, allowing interruptions and distractions, doing the trivial task rather than the hard one (the one that will get results), failure to take responsibility, and getting stuck in planning mode without ever executing or never planning at all.

I can ask someone to tell me what they value and what's important in their life, and they'll get the answer right and give a full list of what's important to them. They may have even set goals; they know what they want to achieve, but their mind unconsciously takes over and foils their efforts. Their hijacker isn't going to budge out of the driver's seat. This is exactly why it's so important for you to understand your own HOS because your hijacker is working very hard to reinforce that unconscious identity that is the foundation of your HOS.

Your Sabotaging HOS

In fact, just when you're *feeling* successful – which is the antithesis of your HOS – that hijacker will work tirelessly to survive by proving that you are, indeed, a failure. Consider these examples of self-sabotaging behaviors exhibited by the various HOS types.

Unlovable: Cannot do what may be right for them because of their intense focus on pleasing other people. For example, an Unlovable doesn't pursue higher education because the spouse isn't willing to take on more household duties and child care. By not being a little selfish, they open the door to being taken advantage of – of course, they do not recognize this – they feel others should pay attention to their needs as much as they do for others. This over-extension of self leads to burnout, resentfulness and eventually, a major blow up in the relationship. They may even get so fed up that "others always take advantage of them," they end a relationship. This further enforces their identity of being Unlovable.

Powerless: Fails to derive satisfaction from a position because it is not at the top of the ladder. If not managed, a Powerless can find themselves continually climbing the corporate ladder into a dissatisfying position – losing sight of better opportunities. It goes without saying that people in positions of power have people who do things for them. Delegation is their game. As a result, they can feel "over entitled" as they get used to others doing for them. Their focus can be so much on getting to the top – they miss out on a more well-rounded life picture.

Incompetent: Get stuck in analysis paralysis and research mode. An Incompetent may miss or pass up a great opportunity simply to avoid being judged as anything less than competent if the endeavor doesn't work out perfectly. They can become overly righteous – which can lead to a closed mind – which can lead to missing out on a real expansion of the mind and potentially, great opportunities or experiences.

Ugly: Can't stop spending on wardrobe, accessories, etc. An Ugly's need to look perfect leads to being late for an important event (think job interview, wedding, etc.) and the tardiness creates lost opportunity or relationship friction or even estrangement. Unfortunately, the clock works against Uglies. Aging is an unavoidable occurrence – one that can be difficult for an Ugly to accept. Details matter, but too much attention on details can overwhelm and even short circuit an Ugly. Another opportunity for self-sabotage is in judging others too harshly for not living up to their "ideal." Judging can be a relationship/friendship killer.

Unlikeable: Cannot stop focusing on ancillary relationships (i.e., constantly adding friends and contacts) to the detriment of the most important relationships in their lives (spouse, family). Spending on others to be deemed more likeable leads to negative financial consequences. Like Unlovables, they can be prone to over-extending themselves and feeling taken advantage of to the point they begin to eradicate friends that don't reciprocate.

Weak: Constantly spending time on physique and the next athletic achievement leads to a relatively shallow life which may later feel "unfulfilling." Their body can also take a beating with extreme workouts. And as much as they would love to be a superhero, superheroes are imaginary. They can become suffocating in relationships.

Dumb: With the need to exhibit their intelligence and that they're the smartest one in the room leads them to continually correct others, a behavior that quickly wears thin with those around them. They easily get bored with small talk unless they work to take a genuine interest in others. They can become so focused on consuming and sharing knowledge that they miss out on really connecting with those around them.

Outcast: FOMO drives every decision. May reject good opportunities because there isn't time in their schedule or they judge the opportunity to be below their standards.

Failure: The need to win at all costs drives decisions. This may lead to lost family time and enjoying kids growing up, regretting it when it's too late. Spending choices are made based on outward appearance rather than value. They may inadvertently fail because they set the bar so high (only to be introduced to someone even more successful) that they truly do fail – as everyone does at one time or another. Another common self-sabotaging behavior is that they find themselves in a very unfulfilling careers or jobs simply because they were chasing financial success instead of fulfillment. The most common sabotaging behavior I see Failures engage in is over spending. They may make a lot of money, but there comes a point when they can actually create greater stress on themselves and family by over-extending themselves financially, thus perpetuating the notion that they are still a failure.

Bad: Constant focus on making things perfect and never deviating from the rules can stifle creativity. By avoiding confrontation, stress builds to a breaking point. They also miss out on enjoyment of life due to the extreme pressure they place on themselves to following the rules, getting it right and making things perfect.

Oddly enough, the ultimate self-sabotaging behaviors show up at the very point we challenge our Human Operating System. The moment we take action or make decisions in "spite" of our HOS is when our identity (aka the hijacker) fights to validate itself. Keep in mind that your Human Operating System is a central element to your identity. By challenging its truth, you set into motion its own survival mechanism.

For example, a Failure may reinforce its identity by over-extending themselves financially and, although they may have gotten to a level of making a lot of money, they bought too many toys, too big a house to hang onto. Losing any "thing" reinforces that they are a failure. Even on a quieter or smaller note, just as you are about to have your best month ever, you take the last day off to shop for your next prize, only to "fall short." Distractions are silent sabotaging behaviors to a Failure. Over-extension is a silent sabotaging behavior to an Unlovable. They can over extend to such a degree that they feel extremely resentful to their partner and breaking it off with them (a common pattern with Unlovables), only to find themselves feeling "unlovable" again.

You and Your Hijacker

Throughout the book, I've blamed your hijacker; however, your hijacker and you are but two sides of the same coin. Your hijacker is the voice in your head that is constantly talking, and his ongoing commentary stream is continuously reinforcing your HOS and his position. It's an insidious stream of thought that often runs on and on unchecked. It drives the choices we make in the instant that can lead to undesired results. It's the voice that makes excuses and finds reasons to support our choices to put our mind at ease, knowing full well the actions are not in our best interest, like the overweight person eating to death and the spender on the way to the poor house. The voice never stops, and that voice is your saboteur.

If you're thinking that you don't have a voice in your head, it's that very thought ("I don't have a voice in my head") that *is* the voice I'm talking about. Some people admit talking to themselves, but whether or not it's admitted or aloud, we all do it. And some people will joke that they answer themselves as well. Truth be told, we all do that in some fashion as well. The voice in your head often both asks and answers questions: "Was I supposed to call my sister? I don't remember. I wonder if I was? She'll be upset if I forgot. I should call her when I get home. I don't want to call her while I'm driving. Oh, I see I need to stop for gas, but it's raining. I wonder if I'll have time tomorrow to get gas. I wonder if the weather will be better tomorrow?" That's the voice.

It is running constantly, so much so that you cannot discern it from the core of **you**. It narrates everything – even when it doesn't need to. You can go for a walk through the park and it is on: "It's a gorgeous day today, a little on the cool side, but nice and sunny. I wonder when it will get hot again? I love hot weather. Maybe I should move somewhere warmer, like Florida. But Florida gets too hot in the summer, I don't know if I could take that heat..." and on, and on it goes.

That voice is like comfortable company. In fact, it can cause discomfort to turn it off. It feels weird and is extremely tough to do. If you have ever tried meditating, you know the challenge I'm speaking of.

The voice can jump from one topic to another with barely a thread of connection, and your thoughts get off on a tangent in a heartbeat. The voice provides a streaming narrative of what you're seeing, and it's the very thing that generates the meaning of everything that happens. The voice isn't who we are, yet it determines our experiences of things, people, and places. Your running narrative is what dictates your emotions – not others. We often blame others for our emotions when, in fact, they have no direct control of our emotions. We make others responsible for our happiness, sadness, success, failure, contentment or anger. As long as we abdicate responsibility of our emotions and outcomes, we are rendered powerless over our situations and experiences. The moment you come to realize that you are directly in control of your outcomes is the moment you have regained the opportunity to direct your life the way you choose. You have taken back control.

More Recognition

Controlling your hijacker and overcoming self-sabotaging behavior is a matter of first recognizing it. You've already recognized and identified your HOS. Now it's time to begin to objectively observe the voice in your head. This is far easier said than done because the voice is the driver of emotions, both good and bad. You are not your voice; you're the one who notices when it's talking. It takes a great deal of practice to begin separating the two and objectively noticing and then managing your voice. For example, if you align with your voice when it says good things about you ("You really nailed that presentation") but dismiss the negative comments ("You are such a klutz"), you have failed to be objective. Yes, we all like nice things said about us; however, keep in mind that you are not your voice, no matter what it says – good or bad. You are you, not the voice in your head.

This may lead you to thinking "Well then, who am I?" That's a very good question. You may not be too familiar with who you are at the core for the shear fact that the voice in your head, a voice conditioned by your environment and directed by your Human Operating

System, has been so insidious that you haven't had a chance to "get to know yourself."

Most of what goes through your head – what your voice says – is meaningless or, worse, self-sabotaging. You may wonder why you have that voice in the first place if it's meaningless or if it tries to thwart your attempts to reach your goals and live the life you truly want. The voice in your head is also the voice that can lead you to fulfilling your goals and aspirations. The voice inside you is an outlet for emotion and its attached energy. Start to pay attention to your voice... not what it says but that it exists at all. Pay attention to the fact that it occurs. Begin to try to separate it from yourself since you are not your voice. Notice how it can alter your attitude and perspective.

Think about two people who have the same experience of a traumatic accident that leads to paralysis. They've suffered the same awful result, but one lives in despair and depression while the other creates a successful business and life of fulfillment despite that same physical limitation. There is an identical experience but with two very different outcomes due to two very different perspectives (or mental narratives). I assure you, the latter example is somehow who has learned to condition and manage the voice in his head.

Begin to simply *notice* the voice rather than listening to what it says. Notice its existence for what it is – a rambling outlet for emotion and energy. As you gain that awareness of the voice, you are setting the stage to manage it. You will become aware of being aware and become conscious of the consciousness itself. It takes work and practice, but try to notice your voice when it's blathering on. Essentially, you begin to think about your thoughts, and that's the first step to taking control.

If you want to "get out of your own way" and stop being "your own worst enemy," you must learn to control and manage the voice. It comes down to mental conditioning and that is at the heart of your HOS. It's a substantial piece to determining experiences, emotions, outlooks, and outcomes! It ultimately circles back to managing your mind, and the first step to managing anything is to recognize and understand it.

For example, when I have a contractor who comes to my house to make a repair, I always want to know what happened and what's needed to fix it. I want to understand what has to happen for the repair, so I need to understand the core of what went wrong in the first place. The same thing is true for my HOS: To use it effectively, the more I understand its inner workings (including a desire for self-sabotage), the more effective I will be at seeing it at work (and objectively seeing the voice for what it is), and then managing it to do what I want rather than the other way around. Only then can I wrest control from the hijacker.

It is then and only then that I can ask, "What am I really committed to here?" This is the opening that allows you to create the ultimate designed outcome for yourself and your life.

Chapter Fifteen:
Managing Your Mind

Having gone through the exercises in the previous chapters and having more insight into how you may be self-sabotaging, you're now at the point at which you recognize your own HOS and better understand the hijacker that's taken over your life. You are also probably very adept at recognizing the HOS of those people in your life including your spouse, siblings, friends, colleagues, etc. I'll also wager that you're also evaluating others with whom you come in contact, and you're probably even pretty good at pegging the HOS of public figures.

The more you recognize the various HOS types, the easier it becomes. The patterns become very obvious because they are so repetitious. As I mentioned at the start, patterns are very telling… about you and about everyone, for that matter. Once you get a handle on it, those patterns are almost impossible to ignore. For me, it has almost become a game: trying to see how quickly I can determine the HOS of anyone.

As with anything you want to manage, recognition is the critical first step. You cannot solve a problem without first understanding what the problem is. The more clearly you recognize and define the problem, the better your solution will be. In this case, the problem is that some precipitating event in your childhood created an operating system within your mind that is a major influencing factor in all of your decision making and which may be preventing you from living the life you truly want. Your hijacker's self-preservation is causing you to repeat patterns of thinking that aren't always in your best interest. Your hijacker is sabotaging your efforts to reach your goals and is sabotaging your life.

I told you at the beginning that the goal is to brainwash your own brain. You will be re-training your brain... your thoughts... to align with what you want. Before we delve into this, I must warn you: It takes work. The best analogy to managing your brain is that of physical fitness. No matter what physical shape you may be in, I'm certain that you understand that one trip the gym, one work out, one brisk walk is not going to get you in top physical condition. The same is true for working out your brain. I want you to equate managing your mind with working out your body.

Your reward for working out your body is a lifetime of improved health, greater physical ability, and quality of life. Working out your mind allows you to live a life that is truly by your design. It ultimately creates the ability for you to direct your income and your personal relationships as well as the lifestyles you choose. The benefits are there so long as you are diligent about doing the work it takes to manage the hijacker within.

You will be re-training your brain. As with physical fitness, the shape you are in right now is a determining factor in how much work you have to put in before you get the results you want. The couch potato who is woefully out of shape will need far more time in the gym to get the desired result than the former athlete who's been out of the game for a few months. The couch potato will probably need months of exercise to reach desired weight and fitness level while the former athlete may only need a few weeks to achieve the same result.

While that's a great metaphor, I find the vast majority of people are mental couch potatoes no matter what sort of physical shape they're in. So don't worry, you've got a lot of company when it comes to the amount of work you will need to put in to re-train your brain, and, I assure you, it's well worth the effort.

Thoughts Abound

When I talk about re-training your brain, I'm talking about managing your thoughts and that inner voice – the voice of your hijacker trying to stay put in the driver's seat, the voice we covered in the last chapter. Stop for a moment to consider all of the random thoughts that run through your brain every minute, every hour, every day.

Consider this scenario that you've no doubt experienced: You wake up feeling refreshed; you're ready to jump out of bed and tackle the day. You have a spring in your step and a smile on your face. You're on fire and jump into the office, thinking about the great things you are going to create or do. Your thoughts are on fire! You will create amazing opportunities for yourself today. Then you get that one call – the upset client who calls to fire you or your spouse texts you, cursing you up and down for **not** remembering that you had promised to take the kids to school today. Suddenly your whole day turns upside down in an instant and the rest of your day is knocked off kilter. Rather than taking this as a single event, your thoughts – that voice – allow it to shape the rest of your day, and that shape is not positive. The smile is gone and your ambition is deflated all because of thoughts you couldn't manage or control, all because the voice kept rambling on negatively. Your mind has been hijacked!

That voice, the narrative, can actually make you paranoid. You lost a client, so now your voice is making you paranoid that your business is going downhill, that it will end up a pile of ashes because you now fear that every other client you have will leave, too. As you sit here reading this, you may be saying (or your voice may be saying), "That is crazy and an over-reaction." And it is. But when it happens to you, your voice starts running that track that you buy into it and your actions, reactions, and emotions are directed as a result.

People tend to equate their thoughts with who they are, and I want you to understand that those two things are not synonymous. You are not your thoughts. You are not the voice in your head. The purpose of learning to manage your mind is to understand how your thoughts can run your emotions… and reactions to events. The more you are able to control the voice and random thoughts, the more effective you become at consciously designing your world including your relationships, lifestyle, and activities.

Here's another scenario that's probably happened to you and illustrates how your thoughts, left to their own devices, will frame an event: You're driving in traffic and get cut off. Your thoughts about that? Your voice goes off: "You jerk. I can't believe you did that. *Insert favorite profanity.*" Your mind tightens. You become negative. You are convinced they are out to get you – to purposely run you off the road. But then… when you pull up alongside that driver at the next light and recognize the person as someone you know, like, and respect, maybe a neighbor or a friend. Suddenly, your mind relaxes again. You realize it wasn't that bad and you probably overreacted. Your reaction to the event is driven by your thoughts –both good and bad. Either way, you are a puppet to them.

Now, that example illustrated just how fast your thoughts, followed by your emotions changed. But in that instance, it happened "by accident." Once you start working out your brain, you will have the ability to shift the direction of your mind on purpose, not just when it happens accidentally from one minute to the next. Managing your thoughts allows you to manage your emotions, which ultimately allows you to manage your actions.

By learning to manage your thoughts and quiet the voice, you can reframe how your mind sees an event. It's just an event, good or bad; however, your thoughts will arise around the event, and your thoughts (good or bad) determine your emotion and reaction. Your mind will always create thoughts around an event because it needs to. Your mind must fill in gaps and create an understanding of the world. The more effective you become at managing your mind, the greater your ability is to create the end result you want. The key is understanding where your mind went during an event.

A simple event – a phone call or being cut off in traffic – can have you in a foul mood because of the uncontrolled thoughts that immediately jump in and take over. Suddenly, you're living the moment, the day, and your entire life at the whim of your thoughts and the voice in your head rather than by the design that you want. The more quickly you notice where your mind went, the faster you can let go of it along with the tension and emotions that resulted.

Puppet or Puppeteer?

Most people don't realize how they are a puppet to their random thoughts. My goal is to change you from being the puppet of your thoughts to being the puppeteer – the one controlling the strings and the outcome. Marcus Aurelius said, "Our life is what our thoughts make it." I want to alter this: Your life is what *you allow* your thoughts to make it. You need to manage your mind first in order to achieve what you want.

> ### *Your life is what you ALLOW your thoughts to make it.*

This probably seems impossible at first because we don't really think about our thoughts. They just happen, and we don't recognize that we're a puppet to these random thoughts that come and go. However, in the same way that you can manipulate a physical movement, you can manipulate your thoughts. You can manipulate your arm and fingers to reach over and pick up a pencil, and you do that consciously. With training, you can manipulate your thoughts to go where you want them to and make them do what you want. You become the puppeteer. You take charge of pulling the strings to control your thoughts rather than the other way around.

Where do thoughts even come from? When you think about the overwhelming randomness of your thoughts, it seems pretty crazy. Your thoughts arise out of conditioning, and that conditioning is driven mostly by your HOS. Your thoughts are habitual, and like any habit, they can be changed. But like all habits, change takes work. The more you work on your mental muscle, the more you will realize how crazy your thoughts are and how crazy it is to let these random thoughts drive your actions and emotions.

The good news is that you are not permanently sentenced to the randomness of your thoughts. You can take control of the puppet strings, but it does take work. You don't go to the gym once and expect to be in great shape. Furthermore, once you get in shape, you must continue to exercise to maintain your physical fitness. The same thing is true for your mental fitness.

In the same way that you had to recognize your HOS to get this far in the process, to become the puppeteer, you have to recognize that thoughts come and go and are truly random and may have no basis whatsoever in reality. To start, begin to recognize thoughts as they come up. For example, if your spouse comes home a few minutes late, where did your mind go regarding that event? What thoughts did you have? Are you upset because they didn't communicate a delayed arrival? Are you beginning to think they're hiding something, perhaps having an affair? It's like your mind went from zero to sixty – a few minutes late to an affair.

Okay, so maybe your mind doesn't go straight to assuming your spouse is having an affair. Maybe your mind went to: "Why is he late? Why doesn't he respect me and my time? He just assumes I should be the one taking care of the kids, making dinner, cleaning up everything while he goes out drinking with his buddies? He just doesn't respect me. My life would be so much better if I was with someone who actually respected me and was more considerate of my time and the effort I put into keeping our home and kids happy and healthy…."

Acknowledge that your mind just made that all up. There was no basis in reality in whatever the thought was that popped up. Your spouse may have just as well been delayed because he or she stopped to pick up ingredients to make dinner. Or got caught in a traffic jam. When thoughts that have no basis in reality pop up, understand where your mind goes by default. Start to take inventory of these thoughts and note the patterns and repetitions. Where do your brain and your thoughts automatically want to go? Does your mind immediately go to the negative possibilities about an event? Do you repeatedly think that people are out to get you? Do you always first think bad things about others? Are you having thoughts about how you appear to others? Worried about what others think about you?

Taking inventory is about stopping when you have a random thought and discerning where it fits. What's your thought pattern? Once you get to this point, you have a greater level of awareness about your mental tendencies. With that awareness, the next time a random thought comes up, you can see it for what it is: a random thought, nothing else, and certainly nothing worth putting much stake into.

Back to the late spouse: When that event happens and random thoughts try to fill in the gaps, stop and see them as random thoughts without a basis in reality. Understand your conditioned pattern of random thoughts based on your inventory. When we create an attachment to the thought, it leads to an emotional reaction and pervasive mood. You'll learn to recognize it and realize, "Wow, that just came out of nowhere. Where did that come from?" Become aware of the randomness of your thoughts.

Awareness leads to the opportunity to manage. If you're not aware of random thoughts, you cannot manage them. The moment you're aware of it, you can manage it. Once you've taken inventory and notice the patterns to which you're typically subjected, you can begin to create an interrupter to that thought pattern. With that interrupter, ask yourself, "What am I really committed to in the moment? Am I committed to being angry, upset, frustrated, down?" Or "Am I committed to taking action, turning this around, creating a great day for myself?" What is your *commitment*?

This interruption allows you the little bit of space you need to assess the thoughts popping up and become very mindful of them. It allows you to shift the direction of your thought pattern. From negative to positive... or at least from perceived negativity to "reality." You consciously take control of your thought pattern. Choosing to become responsible for your outcomes puts you in a position of power. You move from puppet to puppeteer.

Very often, I see someone's inability to interrupt and control a thought pattern from becoming entirely destructive. For example, think about someone who ends up in jail because their emotions got the best of them and they reacted poorly to a situation. Their inability to control their thought process literally sentenced them to jail and the life of being a criminal. It can all happen in an instant. Call it a crime of passion, if you will, but the end result is the same.

Yes, I'll admit that the criminal example is an extreme one; however, the inability to interrupt and redirect thoughts has negative outcomes on many levels. In a personal relationship, you can get frustrated or upset and your thoughts can lead you down a particular path, then you say or do something that can inadvertently destroy a relationship. You'll wish you could take back the words or actions, but you can't.

Your Mind is Busy

Before we go one step further, let me be clear: This is a process. You will develop awareness of your random thoughts and create your inventory over time. You don't simply one day flip a switch and begin to immediately recognize all of this. You don't simply decide when you get up one morning to begin taking inventory of your mind. It doesn't work this way because your mind is very busy paying attention to a lot of different things all at one time... and you have that hijacker who's in no hurry to relinquish control. The voice in your head talks incessantly.

To understand the busyness of your brain, think about driving for a moment. When you're driving, your brain is taking in a lot of stimuli and processing it all. You're paying attention to staying in your lane, watching for other cars coming from any direction, looking at stop lights, street signs, operating the accelerator and brake, remembering your route and final destination. All the while, your mind (and you) are carrying on a dialogue about what happened that day – the conversation you had that morning with your child's teacher which leads you to thoughts about the conversation you need to have with your child that evening. There's a ton going on in your brain, and it's happening without you being completely cognizant of what's going on in your mind. It is all so "normal" to you – the busyness of the mind.

The next step in the process is to begin strengthening the muscle of your mind. A stronger mental muscle leads to a greater consciousness of attention – of the thoughts or "conversations" that arise in your mind. The greater awareness you bring to those thoughts, the faster you catch yourself engaging in them. The faster you can separate yourself from the thoughts, the faster you can take back control of your mind or thoughts.

Creating Stillness

The workout to strengthen the muscle of your mind starts with stillness… or as commonly called, meditation. I'm somewhat hesitant to use that word because many people have a certain pre-existing association with it. You might even have immediately jumped to the idea of "weird philosophy" or religion when you read the word.

Meditation is becoming much more mainstream and is no longer completely associated with the practice of sitting lotus-style with incense burning dressed in monk-like garb. Meditation actually has little or nothing to do with religion. You can add a religious element to it if you choose, but doing so is not necessary to garner the benefit of meditation. Greater numbers of people are embracing the practice, and many companies are now even building or creating meditation rooms for employees because of the many benefits it offers including greater productivity and overall peace of mind.

Very simply, meditation is a matter of being able to settle the constant barrage of information that your mind takes in (and even makes up when it needs to fill in gaps!), so you can sort through all of this information, discern what is relevant and important, dismiss the rest, and regain control of your thoughts.

Your mind is really pretty bad at punctuation. Your thoughts can ramble right along, not stopping, and banging into the next thought in your head. Without needed punctuation, your mind, your thoughts are a jumbled mess. To really illustrate what I mean by this, I've included below a passage from *Tao: The Watercourse Way* by Alan Watts. You may recognize the work and know the story. However, I've also removed all of the punctuation and want you to read this as fast as you can. Fair warning, this will be difficult!

It is almost impossible to give intelligible descriptions of elements or dimensions which are constant in all experiences such as consciousness time motion or electricity yet electricity is very much here having measurable and controllable properties but Professor Harold A Wilson writing on Electricity in the 1947 Encyclopaedia Britannica says *the study of electricity today comprehends a vast range of phenomena in all of which we are brought back ultimately to the fundamental conceptions of electric charge and of electric and magnetic fields these conceptions are at present ultimates not explained in terms of others in the past there have been various attempts to explain them in terms of electric fluids and aethers having the properties of material bodies known to us by the study of mechanics today however we find that the phenomena of electricity cannot be so explained and the tendency is to explain all other phenomena in terms of electricity taken as a fundamental thing the question what is electricity is therefore essentially unanswerable if by it is sought an explanation of the nature of electricity in terms of material bodies* that from a scientist is pure metaphysics change a few words and it would be Saint Thomas Aquinas writing about God yet as I feel it intuitively space and void kung are very much here and every child teases itself out of thought by trying to imagine space expanding out and out with no limit this space is not just nothing as we commonly use that expression for I cannot get away from the sense that space and my awareness of the universe are the same and call to mind the words of the Ch'an Zen Patriarch Huineng writing eleven centuries after Lao-tzu *the capacity of mind is broad and huge like the vast sky do not sit with a mind fixed on emptiness if you do you will fall into a neutral kind of emptiness emptiness includes the sun moon stars and planets the great earth mountains and rivers all trees and grasses bad men and good men bad things and good things heaven and hell they are all in the midst of emptiness the emptiness of human nature is also like this* thus the yin yang principle is that the somethings and the nothings the ons and the offs the solids and the spaces as well as the wakings and the sleepings and the alternations of existing and not existing are mutually necessary how one might ask would you know that you are alive unless you had once been dead how can one speak of reality or is ness except in the context of the polar apprehension of void thus the yin yang principle is that the somethings and the nothings the ons and the offs the solids and the spaces as well as the wakings and the sleepings and the alternations of existing and not existing are mutually necessary how one might ask would you know that you are alive unless you had once been dead how can one speak of reality or is ness except in the context of the polar apprehension of void Yang and yin are in some ways parallel to the later Buddhist view of form se and emptiness k'ung of which the Hridaya Sutra says that which is form is just that which is emptiness and that which is emptiness is just that which is form this seeming paradox is at once intelligible in terms of the idea of clarity ch'ing for we think of clarity at once as translucent and unobstructed space and as form articulate in every detail as what photographers using finely polished lenses call high resolution and this takes us back to what Lao-tzu said of the usefulness of doors and windows through perfect nothing we see perfect something In much the same way philosophers of the Yin-Yang School 3rd century saw the positive and negative as aspects of t'ai chi the Great Ultimate initially represented as an empty circle as wu chi although chi seems to have had the original meaning of a ridgepole upon which of course the two sides of a roof yang and yin would lean the yin-yang principle is not therefore what we would ordinarily call a dualism but rather an explicit duality expressing an implicit unity the two principles are as I have suggested not opposed like the Zoroastrian Ahura Mazda and Ahriman but in love and it is curious that their traditional emblem is that double helix which is at once the pattern of sexual communication and of the spiral galaxies *One yin and one yang is called the Tao The passionate union of yin and yang and the copulation of husband and wife is the eternal pattern of the universe if heaven and earth did not mingle whence would everything receive life t*he practical problem of life was not to let their wrestling match get out of hand only recently have the Chinese set their hearts upon some kind of utopia but this must be understood as the necessary reaction to years and years of foreign exploitation anarchy and extreme poverty but in the 4th century Chuang-tzu wrote *thus those who say that they would have right without its correlate wrong or good government without its correlate misrule do not apprehend the great principles of the universe nor the nature of all creation one might as well talk of the existence of Heaven without that of Earth or of the negative principle without the positive which is clearly impossible yet people keep on discussing it without stop such people must be either fools or knaves*

Whew! Did it make any sense at all? Perhaps at the beginning. Or maybe a few snippets here and there. Mostly, it was a jumbled mess, right? You may have already experienced this confusion when reading email or a post from someone who failed to use punctuation or chose not to because of Twitter's character count limit... or plain ol' laziness when typing. To be honest, you may have found yourself, like most people, not even being able to finish reading it.

This is a good exercise to illustrate what happens to your mind when you don't give it the punctuation it needs. In order for this literary passage, this book, or any written communication to make sense, you need punctuation. For that matter, you need punctuation – or at least the pauses it represents – when speaking as well. Try telling someone something without the natural pauses that do and must occur in speech and see if they can understand what you're talking about. Or think about how someone who's excited communicates – rapidly and with few if any pauses. What is the typical reaction to that? "Slow down."

This rapid-fire, no punctuation approach is what your brain does all... day... long. You don't realize that it's happening because you've habituated to it. You've tuned out because it's overloaded circuits in your brain – higher level circuits that lead to your best thinking. There is a constant barrage of stimuli coming at us from the moment we open our eyes every morning: conversations; tasks to be done; input from television, radio or other media; billboards and the daily onslaught of advertising that reaches us; and the list goes on.

It's exactly like being in a noisy situation. At first it's a distraction, but after a while, you can tune it out because you habituate to it. Think about a vacuum cleaner running. It starts as noise and you can acknowledge that it's loud and annoying, but after a certain length of time, you don't really notice it any longer. But it's still running. The noise is still there, but your mind became accustomed to it and tuned it out. This is what is happening inside our heads – the thoughts are still flowing through constantly, but we can't really discern them. We get accustomed to all the "noise" going on in our heads and can't pick out one thought from the next. It's those pages of text without a comma, period, semicolon, or question mark to create meaning and logic.

Meditation or stillness begins to train our brains to put the punctuation back in where it belongs. If I put the punctuation back into that passage you read, it would make sense to you. Our minds become very dirty and mucky if we don't do this. The jumbled mess of our thoughts can continue to pile up. It can easily become physically stressful.

Getting Started

Think back to the analogy of going to the gym to get back in shape. It's important that you start working out correctly. In fact, depending on your condition, you may even need to see a doctor before starting an exercise regimen. If you've been down this road, you know that if you start by trying to do too much at the outset, you are setting yourself up for failure. Let's say you decide to get in better shape, so you hit the gym and choose to do an hour-long aerobics class followed by strenuous weight training and wrap up the session with 30 minutes on the elliptical machine.

Chances are excellent that you'll be so sore the next day that not only do you not want to return to the gym, simply getting out of bed might feel impossible. Not at all the way you should start. Instead, you'll start by walking on the treadmill for 15 minutes. The next day, perhaps you'll add five more minutes and continue to increase the duration incrementally. After a week or two of that, you'll add some weight training. You get the picture.

The same thing is true with starting the exercises you need to do to manage your mind, what I'll call stillness. To start, take five minutes, just five minutes, to quiet your mind. The most important aspect of this, as with any sort of physical exercise, is consistency! You don't have to dedicate long periods of time to stillness, but it has to be consistent and daily.

So what do you do in these five minutes? You want to achieve stillness of your mind, emptying it of random thoughts. There are plenty of podcasts to guide you through this process. (I've included some of my favorites in the

Resource section in the back of this book.) You'll definitely want to use one of these podcasts or a similar device; otherwise, you'll notice how quickly your random thoughts start racing in and taking over the stillness you're trying to achieve! Don't believe that? Go ahead and, on your own, try to empty your mind of random thoughts. I guarantee the voice in your head will take over saying, "Oh my gosh, this is so hard. This seems like such a long time. How can I do this every day?" Or "I'm too busy to do this right now!" "I just don't have the time."

It's amazing how 30 different thoughts can enter your mind in as many seconds. Like I said, your mind is busy and is always running through random thoughts. When you have someone else guiding your mind (through one of these podcasts, for example), it provides a place for your mind and thoughts to return to. It gives you something on which to focus to generate stillness in your mind.

As with exercise, you'll work up to longer periods of time. Start with five minutes daily for a week or two to get in the habit. Then slowly add more time, even just an additional minute or two. Before long, you'll be at ten, then 15 minutes. Scientifically, it's been proven that there is tremendous value if you can work your way to 20 minutes a day. Now before you immediately have a knee-jerk reaction thinking that you can't imagine carving out 20 more minutes for something else in your already busy day, remember that I said five minutes to start. Use five minutes of your lunch break, or take a five-minute break mid-morning or mid-afternoon. You're probably already taking that break, so do something constructive for yourself rather than water cooler chat or perusing social media.

Once you've been doing this consistently, you will notice that your mind starts to crave this stillness. You'll actually be looking forward to this period of time when you're able to shut off the hyper-stimulus of your mind. Again, equating this to physical activity: Your body is designed for activity and movement; however, even the best athletes need to take a break and rest. Your body cannot keep going and going and going. Without needed rest, your physical capabilities diminish. After a rest, you're ready to go again.

Once you recognize that your mind already finds ways to shut down throughout the day, like a mistreated or over-run engine seizing up, by "killing time" browsing the internet, going shopping or watching television, you'll understand the need for stillness. The mind will trick you into believing that what you are doing at the moment is important, but in reality, it is inadvertently seeking ways to tune out. When you take a few minutes to meditate, it is almost like taking a quick nap – refreshing your mind to allow it to think at a high level again.

What you probably haven't realized is that, like your body, your mind cannot keep going and going and going, but it tries to do this anyway. Your mind's efforts to keep going are those jumbled, random thoughts without punctuation that have been conditioned to cause you to react and become emotional about daily events. Your mind's effort to keep going is driven by your hijacker. Once you give your mind a time of stillness, you will understand that your mind actually craves a break the same way your body craves a break when you're exerting for extended periods.

During stillness, close your eyes to shut off all visual stimuli. After your five-minute period of stillness, when you first open your eyes, you'll notice how vibrant things are again and how clear your mind feels. Those jumbled thoughts create a certain muckiness in your mind, and once you begin practicing consistent stillness, you'll realize how this process helps clean and clear your brain.

Truthfully, you can't effectively manage your mind without going through this exercise consistently. You have to be wholeheartedly committed to wanting to manage the outcome, your emotions, your reactions. You must be committed to the intended outcomes of your relationships, your business, your parenting skills. The exercise of consistent daily stillness will allow you to see things you couldn't see before.

For example, let's say you have a child who's acting out. You get frustrated by him or her and it's exhausting; however, without having a clear mind and the perspective that comes with that and achieved through stillness, you will not be able to unravel and decode the real message behind the behavior. I tell you that from my own experience.

When my daughter was two and half, we began having challenges with the morning routine, and it was an exhausting way to start the day. Everything was an effort. She worked against everything I tried to do. Even just trying to get a sock on her foot became an impossibility. I would get one sock on, she would take it off. It was like, "Oh, you've got to be kidding me!" After a few days of this, I had to stop my mind from heading toward the frustrating thoughts of thinking about how much power this toddler was exerting. How much power could... or should... a two-and-a-half year old have over an adult? I had to stop myself and ask what was really going on. And though I felt like doing it, yelling at her was not the answer. The only reason I was able to stop and assess the situation was because I recognized what was happening in my mind and with my thought process.

Had I not been aware of the way the mind likes to work, the frustration would have taken over, and her acting out would have continued to feed the frustration, and the whole thing would start to spiral out of control. The more frustrated I got, the more she acted out. I stopped and took inventory of what was happening and asked why a two-and-a-half year old would suddenly start doing this. Aside from wanting to exhibit some independence... and being two... there had to be something else driving this new behavior, seemingly out of the blue.

Then I realized my daughter had just been put into a new pre-school for the second time that summer with a whole new set of strangers, strange kids, and strange teachers in a strange place. Once I put myself in her shoes, I gained a whole new level of empathy about what she was dealing with and going through. As a result, I began talking with her about it in the morning: How proud I was of her for being so brave, how great she was to be able to meet new friends, how there was an opportunity to play with new toys there. Then at the end of the day, if she had a really great day... we celebrated with ice cream, her favorite thing in the world. No kidding, it took just two days of this, and she was an entirely different kid!

Had I not taken the time to stop and think about my thoughts and eliminate the "noise of every day," my frustration and the random thoughts that would infiltrate my mind would have continued, and I would have completely missed what was really happening. Would I have eventually figured it out? Maybe. But it is far better to figure it out and correct it sooner than later, before little issues become big problems.

Just Start

There are two pitfalls around creating stillness in your mind. First and most likely, you're going to get caught up in thinking that you are too busy to do this as I mentioned earlier. Secondly, you're going to get frustrated because *this is hard to do*. It's exactly like deciding to go to the gym to get in better shape. First, you have to find time to go, and second, it's easy to become frustrated when you don't see results immediately or that just a few minutes on the treadmill is so challenging! So you start with a 20-minute workout and you realize that 20 minutes one time isn't going to get you in shape, but it's a start… and you have to start someplace. It will take consistency of 20 minutes every day and building on that.

Accept the fact that it's going to be tough to start. Embrace it as a challenge. Look at it as an exercise in building the muscle of your will (think will power). Pick a time during the day when you can consistently devote five minutes and work your way up. You're certainly not limited to five minutes, but you have to dedicate at least five minutes to start. Perhaps, like me, you find yourself getting tired in the mid-afternoon. Or times when you feel crazy busy and really scattered. That may seem like a counterintuitive time to take a break for stillness, but it's actually a great time. Once you have your thoughts quieted, you'll be able to better manage the craziness that may be around you. You'll notice that day after day, it gets easier and easier (just like exercise), so you can add more time. Before you know it, you will notice that it is now just a part of your daily routine.

The beginning part of stillness is just shutting off those thoughts that want to pop up. This enables you to better recognize how often these thoughts pop up, see them for what they are, and let them go. During stillness, you are practicing shutting off these thoughts, so that you're better able to do the same thing during other parts of your day. You are conditioning yourself and your brain to shut off useless thoughts automatically.

Next, you want to gain comfort with having no thoughts for a period of time. Let the brain activity settle. This may sound simple, but remember: your mind has been an ongoing constant jumble of thoughts and you've habituated to having all of those thoughts running through your brain. Having no thoughts actually takes practice.

I equate developing a comfort to shutting off the mind with shutting off the television. You probably know someone (or perhaps that someone is you), that must have the television on **all the time**. They walk in the door and the first thing they reach for is the remote. They don't necessarily sit down to actually **watch** the television, but they need the background noise to feel "comforted." The background noise is synonymous with the background noise in the brain. Just as it is uncomfortable to the person who must have the TV on all the time, it can be a bit uncomfortable (at first) to stop the ongoing stream of thoughts in your brain.

The third step is beginning to consciously plug in the programming that you want to put in your brain. This is where mantras come into play. Your mantra becomes the thing that you want to focus your attention on when random thoughts pop up. Your mantra is a reminder of the important stuff rather than the random thoughts or the negative thoughts if that has typically been your pattern. Repeating a mantra is conscious conditioning. It is a statement that focuses your attention on what will benefit the mind. This doesn't have to be anything like, "Honor the divinity within myself" or a similar mantra. It could be something simpler like, "I'm committed to having an effective day" or "I'm committed to having a great relationship."

This is the point at which you are re-training your brain. Rather than going to negative thoughts when an event happens, you replace that with something more positive. You recondition yourself and your mind to look for an opportunity rather than seeing a problem. If you're a pervasive pessimist, this is what can help you become more of an optimist. It trains your brain to recognize opportunities or create solutions. When your mind can identify solutions to challenges, you will have more confidence in more positive outcomes. This leads you to looking forward to what is around the corner instead of fearing it. It simply helps you design and stick to your ultimate outcomes.

Again, it is work, but the benefits are real. As mentioned, use a podcast mentioned in the Resource section (or find another one that suits you) and start with five minutes. If you didn't know the first thing about working out, you'd turn to a trainer to help you get started. That person will guide you correctly through the exercises and equipment, so you can get the physical results you want. The same thing is true with a meditation podcast. With it, you'll get the guidance you need on learning to quiet the mind and achieve stillness. It is not something you can simply do. While it seems like it should be, it is something you need to learn.

While I've stressed that this takes work and commitment, it is something you must do. Most importantly, the whole point of this is to begin to put yourself back in the driver's seat of your world, so it turns out the way you choose!

Chapter Sixteen:
Embrace Your Own Human Operating System

By now you have a clear sense of your own HOS, and you have a better understanding of the self-sabotaging behaviors directed by the hijacker in your life. Hopefully you're starting to recognize those behaviors for what they are in the same way that you've come to recognize under which HOS you operate. I also hope you have started (at least started) to work on quieting your mind and your thoughts and are taking the steps needed to stop those thoughts when they start to run rampant through your brain without rhyme or reason. Quieting your mind is an integral part of overcoming any and all self-sabotaging behaviors.

Each HOS has certain negativities associated with it, along with the respective hijacker's self-sabotaging activities that it exhibits for self-preservation and to maintain control – to keep his hands on the steering wheel. These are the things that lead to the problems in our lives and create the obstacles we must all overcome in order to live life by design rather than by default. These are the things that cause us to "stand in our own way." I'm certain it is these problems and obstacles that led you into the pages of this book in the first place! It's the very thing that brings most, if not all, of my clients to my proverbial doorstep.

It is common for my clients who are going through the process of learning about their own Human Operating Systems for the first time to ask if they can "trade it in" for a different one or get rid of it all together. Of course, no one wants to be associated with the negative traits of each Human Operating System. The Unlovable doesn't want to admit troubled relationships; the Powerless doesn't want to confess that everything he does is for one-upmanship; the Incompetent and Failure don't want to plead guilty to the fear of bombing; the Unlikeable and the Outcast don't want to admit their need for the party or fitting in; the Ugly doesn't want to seem shallow. None of them, not the Weak, the Dumb, and the Bad want to align themselves with the negative traits associated with each of those HOS types. That makes total sense.

However, despite the associated negativity with each HOS, the last thing you want to do is actually get rid of it! Recall the metaphor I used when initially describing what an HOS is and how it works. It is essentially the underlying operating system of a computer. Without an operating system, the computer is useless. No software or apps will run. Heck, even the simple clock becomes functionless. Like a computer, you have to have an operating system.

Trade it in for another? Why? Perhaps some of the negative traits of the other HOS types don't seem as bad to you as yours? The reality is your HOS is an area of your life that has maintained great focus and practice over the years; you have been practicing how to be proficient at the traits and skill sets that represent the opposite of the Human Operating System. In thinking about your profession and career, I doubt you would want to discard the years you have invested in learning your business or trade and the experience you now have as a result. You wouldn't want to do that with your HOS either.

The silver lining is that every single HOS type brings with it certain gifts. Yes, gifts. These are your proficiencies, strengths, "natural" abilities. These are the areas in each HOS that has had hyper-focus throughout a person's entire life. That's a lot of learning. For some of you, it's decades. As a result, your hijacker is quite savvy. The goal isn't to kick him out of the car. The goal is to move him over to the passenger seat or the back seat while you take control of the steering wheel. You can leverage the years of practice that your hijacker has and use that to your advantage. You can receive valuable input from the hijacker, but ultimately you are in control of the vehicle and where it goes.

Insomuch as we all have blind spots and may fail to see our own self-sabotaging behavior, it's also easy to be unable to perceive our natural skill sets. I say "natural skill sets"; however, they aren't necessarily natural. They have been cultivated through many years of focus, practice, and investment even though you have possibly been unaware of that happening.

Now it's time to embrace your HOS and focus on its positive aspects, so you can use it to your advantage.

The Benefits of Each HOS

Having read this far and gone through the earlier exercises, you should be clear about which HOS you have. Perhaps you still don't want to admit to it yet because of the negative association it has, so let's look at all of the positive aspects of the various HOS types. If you still need more help discerning which one is yours, there is additional support at www.TheHijacker.net.

The Unlovable has a strong ability to connect with others. This person excels at making others feel important, taken care of, and safe. There is a great deal of trust because it is imperative for a relationship to exist. Unlovables are the "caregivers," either figuratively or literally. The world needs caregivers.

The Powerless has the ability to command the troops. The Powerless acts in terms of the mission to accomplish. Whatever the mission may be, it becomes the focus and the goal. This person has the ability to create a following and influence others. They are great enrollers and are the "generals."

The Incompetent does things and does them well. The Incompetent is a fact finder and task accomplisher. They strive to get it "right." Incompetents are the "fixers." They don't like to leave things or people "broken." They are reliable and helpful.

The Ugly makes an excellent coordinator. This person has a great eye for coordination both physically (e.g., fashion) and for events. These people make tremendous event planners. Planning a wedding or other milestone celebration? Hire an Ugly. They are the "pretty makers." Also, because they have a keen eye for detail, they also make good client service coordinators.

For the Unlikeable, people like to be in their company. They are great networkers and are simply enjoyable people to be around. Unlikeables are often offered favors and support because they provide that to others. They are the "proverbial salesmen" and "connectors."

For the Weak, strength is an asset. They are strong protectors. They are the "bodyguards."

The Dumb is the "brainiac." These are super smart people who are good with words and/or numbers. They are excellent researchers and are often noted resources. They have the patience to get the answer. Need a go-to person for information? Find a Dumb.

The Outcast is the "socialite." These are the people you see in every local magazine featuring all the happenings and events around town. Somehow they manage to be everywhere, in the mix, all the time. Everyone knows their name.

The Failure is hands-down, without-a-doubt successful. Their driven, never-give-up mentality breeds success. That success trickles down. Think job creation and similar benefits to others across the board. Failures are often the innovators, and they turn ideas into reality.

The Bads are the good-natured, trustworthy ones. They are the "old reliables" among us. Bads are tried and true, always there and hard-working... When living a balanced life, they are good role models.

Leveraging Applications

In addition to recognizing the benefits and attributes of your own HOS, you should also think about situations and circumstances in which you can leverage those to your advantage and, perhaps, situations to avoid because your HOS may cause you to stumble. You have different strengths and weaknesses tied to your HOS; we all do.

Embracing the strengths and recognizing the weaknesses will help you prosper.

Take someone who is Powerless. A Powerless who understands how to leverage his HOS will recognize that he is at his best when he's in front of the room, in charge of the presentation, especially if he is being backed by someone in the audience giving him a testimonial. It puts him in a position of power by being the expert at the front of the room. He does great in this situation. He thrives and prospers. However, send this same person off to a networking event where there is a lot of one-on-one interaction and conversation, and… well, he won't succeed as well because there is no position of power. He would be outside of his "area of proficiency."

On the other hand, if we send an Unlikeable to that same networking event, he'll thrive and will likely come away with dozens of contacts and even more business cards. This arena plays right into the hand of the Unlikeable.

It's important to remember that neither one of these people is necessarily better than the other. They simply have different strengths. Both can advance their careers, relationships, and lives by recognizing and utilizing those strengths and having a clear understanding of the situations in which they will excel… and those in which they may struggle.

As another example, a Dumb may make a great author based on their existing wisdom or insatiable desire to learn what they may not know. Authorship plays right into the Dumb's desire to be recognized for their intelligence and for what they know. Conversely, an

Incompetent may not make the best author in the world, but they'll shine as an editor or proofreader. The Incompetent will thrive on fixing typos, correcting grammatical mistakes, and getting the facts straight.

Recognizing your HOS along with its detriments and attributes will allow you to rein in the former and capitalize on the latter, so you can achieve that which you want in your life, that which you design. By doing so, you move the hijacker out of the driver's seat and into the passenger seat where he belongs. Keep in mind that he's had a lot of practice and may offer you some navigational expertise that you can now use to your advantage. It's okay to allow him to do that, but you really have to wrest control from him, so you're in the driver's seat and can get where you want to go. You can't live without an HOS, but you can make it work for you rather than against you.

Exercise:

List three to five examples of times when you had your highest levels of success. Ask yourself:

- What do all of these examples have in common?
- What situations or specifics do they share?
- How do they relate to your HOS?
- How could you leverage this knowledge to help you excel in your business?
  - Your relationships?
  - Your finances?

Whatever it is you look to accomplish, there are always a number of different paths to achieve it. When we are armed with the knowledge of how we work best, we can use the appropriate formula to help us succeed more consciously without destroying other areas of our lives in the process. Conscious attention is the key to creating your ideal business and or life design.

Chapter Seventeen:
Your HOS and Your Relationships

The real benefit of understanding various Human Operating Systems – your own as well as those of the other people in your life – is how they can and do impact your relationships. With that understanding comes the ability to manage, and management can ultimately lead to improving our relationships with those around us. As I've suggested throughout this book, there's effort needed to uncover your own HOS, to recognize your own self-sabotaging behavior, and certainly to learn to manage and quiet your mind. There is effort needed to move your hijacker out of the driver's seat, but that effort pays off!

Having rewarding relationships around us creates a more fulfilling life. In my experiences, those who hate their business, generally do so because they dislike their relationships. Discontentedness at home is generally due to the fact that the relationship with a spouse or kids is a mess. I'm sure there are very few people who desire to create the life of their own design simply to live it as a hermit, without others with whom to share it. This chapter is intended to help you apply what you've learned about Human Operating Systems and understand the vital needs of your most important relationships – both in your own actions and your reactions to others.

One critical caveat to this chapter is that relationships are highly complex and are very difficult to simplify in a single chapter. There may, one day, be a sequel – an entire book – devoted specifically to this topic alone, but for now, I believe it's important to at least scratch the surface, so you have a bit of insight about the impact that each of our HOS types has on one another. I felt the book would be incomplete if I ignored this concept simply because it can get quite complicated. So, yes, you will find that some of the examples may be a bit simplified; however, I believe you will also find that each of the overviews is quite accurate as well, and I also think that you will quickly see yourself or your spouse, friends, or co-workers, in some of the examples.

Certainly one of the most important relationships in your life is the one with your spouse or partner. It's the most intimate relationship any of us can have. It can create a very exciting life if it is in alignment, or it can be the source of unfulfilled dreams or endless consternation. While you can apply the impact that HOS's have in relationships, I will be focusing this chapter and its examples on the relationship between significant others. That said, once you see the relationship impacts of Human Operating Systems in that very close relationship, the same information and understanding can then be easily extrapolated and applied to the relationships you have with family, friends, and co-workers.

Unlovable

If being showered with attention and adoration are your thing (and to be honest, who doesn't want that?), then an Unlovable is a great person to be with. Unlovables go out of their way to ensure that others' needs are always being met. The downside to this is that, often, their own needs go unmet.

If you don't realize you are with an Unlovable, you could fall into the trap of taking all that they have to give for granted. When working with clients, I often hear, "She loves doing those things for others. It's just the way she is." While this is certainly true of an Unlovable, it almost seems to excuse the need of the recipients of this attention from "giving back." Unlovables will give and give and give until they can't give anymore. They want to make sure that others feel good about themselves and are happy when they are with them.

However, most Unlovables never ask for what **they** want or need – they feel it is selfish. This can be a major trap or pitfall... for you and for them. Unlovables can quickly become resentful for doing so much for others and not getting much back. If you don't consciously recognize that Unlovables also have their own needs (despite the fact that they do not often vocalize them), then you could quickly become the enemy. And you **do not** want to become the enemy of an Unlovable. They are extremely loyal and loving... until they're not.

In other words, when they feel slighted, taken for granted or unappreciated, they become extremely angry and resentful. Unlovables are somewhat known for "losing it." Because they swallow their pride for others, pay attention to others, do for others **all the time**, there can come a breaking point for them. Everyone has a breaking point. That breaking point doesn't necessarily come fast, but it comes hard and seemingly "out of the blue" and may be unrepairable.

If you are an Unlovable, you need to be aware of your own failure to share and ask for what you need and want, politely and diplomatically, of course. And you must communicate this long before you reach your breaking point. When working with Unlovables, I coach them to begin to speak up when something is still just a small frustration, before it has had a chance to fester into deep-seated anger and resentment. This is a difficult challenge for the Unlovable, but one that is vital to the future success of rewarding relationships.

Meet the emotional needs of an Unlovable and you have a partner for life. Show appreciation for how they go out of their way for you and for others (perhaps your children). Ask what you can do for them, and do not take "nothing" for an answer. Sometimes, you'll need to pull it from them and assure them that having their own needs met is not an act of selfishness. This small action will mean the world to an Unlovable, even if they might resist it.

On the other hand, take their giving nature for granted and lose them for life!

Powerless

Keep in mind that it is in the DNA that someone with the Powerless HOS be "powerful." Unless they have done a lot of personal development (and even then it could still be a challenge), the Powerless have a need to be the "leader of things." For some, it may seem that the obvious by-product would be someone who is in ultimate control of the household. However, keep in mind that most leaders do not like to *do* everything. They like to *lead* to certain outcomes and have others do the "doing" as long as they have input into the decisions. Menial tasks around the house can be "beneath" them. Paying someone to do the menial tasks is more their preference.

Telling a Powerless "what" to do can rub them raw. Instead, asking them how and when they can get to something is a better approach. The upside is that the Powerless value the team concept. Just because they like to lead does not mean that they do not value input. In fact, they value it greatly. It is critical that the significant other to a Powerless recognizes that a Powerless can short circuit if they feel circumvented.

For example, if a Powerless is going out to meet with friends, it can anger them to "tell" them when you need them home. A better approach is to ask them when they plan to be home, to let them know what is happening, and that you would need them home by a certain time. Consider posing it this way: "Honey, when do you think you will be home tonight? I am exhausted and will need help putting little Joey to bed. Could you be home by his bedtime?" Team input, explaining the need, and making the request is an effective sequence.

Powerless inherently have a need to be acknowledged. In the corporate world, acknowledgement comes in the form of higher levels of seniority, higher pay rates, bigger offices and so on. At home, this acknowledgement can occur in the form of recognizing and praising outcomes and asking for input. Verbal affirmation is an ideal way to "feed" the needs of a Powerless.

As someone who is Powerless and in a relationship, be aware of the fact that not all spouses enjoy being in a subservient role. They usually want to be a real partner who shares in the direction and decisions in the household. It is rare to find someone who wants to be *doing* everything it takes to run a household, so while it may feel like menial work compared to the important job you do at the office, it is imperative to keeping the peace (and ultimately) the success of your number one relationship.

Incompetent

Incompetents like control. They want to be recognized for their abilities, and they want to get things done – usually done according to their own specifications. They can be narrowly focused on the "right way to do things."

If you are in a relationship with an Incompetent, you won't necessarily get very far or score many points by complimenting their appearance. Instead, compliment their abilities. To an even greater degree, to score points with an Incompetent, instead of only paying lip service about how well they do things, put your money where your mouth is and offer to help. Incompetents typically become angry because they feel like they are the ones who have to do everything (think household chores, for example).

However, tread a bit lightly here since Incompetents tend to have an ingrained notion along the lines of "If I want it to be done right, I have to do it myself." When offering to pitch in to help, you'll certainly gain favor with an Incompetent by asking *how* they would accomplish the task and then proceeding to do it their way. On the flip side, if you are an Incompetent, you'll benefit your own relationship(s) by accepting that there is usually more than one way to "skin the proverbial cat," and your relationship is far better served if you focus on the result (carpet is cleaned) rather than the effort (vacuuming in a different direction than you might choose). Complimenting your spouse for folding the laundry, rather than correcting them on *how* it should be folded. Some battles are not worth fighting…. This is a tough lesson for Incompetents.

For Incompetents, they demonstrate value in the relationship by "doing," and they can be far too laser focused on the doing without taking time to relax and enjoy. In my own case, when my husband suggests we spend three hours on a Saturday on the boat, my immediate thought goes to all the tasks related to the boat, like cleaning, upkeep, and maintenance… rather than simply spending time relaxing!

If you're in a relationship with an Incompetent, you'll have to encourage them to relax and enjoy instead of always doing, but that may take some scheduling compromises. Perhaps Saturdays are for the tasks and the to-do list, and Sundays are for play.

Ugly

For the Ugly, yes, appearances matter. However, it goes far beyond simply being all about appearances. It's about the details and coordination as well. Even the household schedule is important because that plays right into the importance of details. Their decisions are driven by details, one of which is the attention to their appearances.

Consider the Ugly who takes great pains to coordinate a Friday schedule and itinerary, sharing responsibilities to pick up children from school and take them to various after-school practices and the school dance with time for a short but romantic dinner squeezed in the middle. Yes, the Ugly can coordinate this seemingly crazy schedule, but when her husband drops the ball and arrives 15 or 30 minutes late for one aspect of his responsibility, it derails the entire thing, and romantic dinner turns into anything but. His failure to honor the schedule makes her insane.

If you are an Ugly, work to understand that your attention to detail may be too extreme in some instances, and you are probably the only person who will notice when one "i" is left undotted or one "t" left uncrossed.

While the Ugly takes the time she perceives she needs to make everything perfect (appearance and details), complaining that it takes too long is simply greasing the path to conflict. Yes, Uglies want compliments on appearance, especially when they put extreme effort into looking good – and these are compliments offered without asking or needing to prod for it – but they also want to be acknowledged for the effort, not simply the result.

Consider, from the Ugly's perspective, the diametric difference between these two statements:

"You look beautiful even without any makeup."

"You look beautiful."

If you're in a relationship with an Ugly, opt for the latter every time.

Unlikeable

Socializing is paramount in the world of the Unlikeable. It's critical to honor the Unlikeable's need to connect. Conversely, if you are an Unlikeable, it's important to step back and understand that not everyone has the same intense need to connect. An Unlikeable has to realize that just because their partner or spouse doesn't like to go out every night of the week does not make them a boring person.

If you're with an Unlikeable, accept that it's this need for connection and socialization that provides their "juice." Trying to thwart this would be like trying to keep an extrovert in a box, and that never works well.

They thrive on paying attention to others, and that attention can often be misconstrued by a partner or spouse. If you have an Unlikeable as your partner, it's very important not to be jealous or self-conscious when your Unlikeable wants to connect with others. The ones with this HOS type aren't minimizing their relationships with their spouses in wanting to connect with others – they simply want *all* of the connections. In the mind of the Unlikeable, the desire for all connections does not mean that all connections are equal and that the spouse has a lower priority. In fact, their spouse is important and they typically want their spouse to be a part of their activities.

Managing the social calendar is critical in honoring an Unlikeable. If you are an Unlikeable, you need to be sensitive to the potential for your spouse's misunderstanding about his or her priority in your life. Sometimes, you just have to pay attention to the one person you're with. For example, this is very important on date night. Date night is for the two of you to connect, not for you to invite five of your closest friends to join you on your "date."

Conversely, if you are with an Unlikeable, you have to engage in his or her social world as well and be part of it.

In doing so, keep in mind the Unlikeables need to be the center of attention and desire to be adored. Also, give them the opportunity and space to make others feel special. This is what makes the world go around for Unlikeables.

Weak

For a Weak, time for physical activity is a priority – they'll need their time at the gym... period. Also, the Weaks' activities trend toward the outdoors. Understand that a Weak will never be someone who sits on the couch all day, and a match between a Weak and a couch potato will certainly have more than its share of daily challenges. Couch potato tendencies will never resonate with a Weak. A Weak will see this as a character flaw.

To enhance your relationship with a Weak, you should acknowledge their strength and their need to protect. This is the very foundation of their own sense of self-worth. You have to understand their need to protect, even when you personally deem it unnecessary and even when it can get annoying. Someone who is the proverbial "damsel in distress" would make a very good partner for a Weak. This person likes to be protected and the Weak likes to protect. Match made in heaven, so to speak. On the flip side, if someone can handle themselves very well (i.e., an Incompetent), they might become annoyed with a Weak... oil and water. Or worse, gasoline and a flame.

If you're with a Weak, accept and understand their need to protect, and this should be acknowledged as their way of caring and showing love.

Dumb

If your partner or spouse is a Dumb, start by stroking the intelligence ego. In fact, be cognizant of the fact that Dumbs typically have very sensitive egos.

The Dumb is driven to share their knowledge. If you fall into this HOS type, work to stay aware of the need to give *others* space to share, talk, and engage. Recognize and acknowledge that you can be easily bored in a conversation that is not up to your perceived level, so try to be patient. It is important for a Weak to recognize that others (even if the IQ of the other person is a few points below them), have a lot to offer to a conversation.

If you're with a Dumb, work in activities that engage the brain. For example, going to a speaker series or educational presentation makes a lot of sense for date night. Look for things that will stimulate new and different conversations. To keep the fires stoked in a relationship with a Dumb, think about expanding yourself (e.g., reading a new book or even asking for reading recommendations) in order to elevate the conversations you have and to continually have something to contribute to the quest for knowledge, encouraging the Dumb to want to pay attention.

Patience on the part of both the Dumb and the partner is a critical component of relationship success.

Outcast

It's all about inclusion, inclusion, inclusion… and acceptance. Accept their uniqueness and what it is about them that makes them human. Keep in mind that for the Outcast, fitting in is critical, so pointing out anything that may be odd, different, weird, or wrong about them is lighting the match that will cause the relationship to explode.

Honor who they are at their core. Don't incessantly try to change them or make them "normal" according your standards or judge them for not fitting in like everybody else. If they're boisterous, let them be boisterous. If they have tattoos up and down their arms, so be it. Their uniqueness as an individual is likely what you found so intriguing about them in the first place, so honor it instead of making it wrong.

The odd thing about those with an Outcast HOS, in terms of their hijacker's need for self-preservation of identity, is that to be cast out, although uncomfortable, cuts to the core of an Outcast. It's almost an expectation of theirs. If you don't accept them for who they are, it's very easy for them to say, "Screw you"… and walk away.

If you're in a relationship with an Outcast, remember that from their perspective, they may feel the need to compete to fit in with you. Consider what it is about them – what aspect of their uniqueness – that first attracted you and continually acknowledge and embrace that. Keep them in the loop about what is going on and you'll always be on their good side.

If you are an Outcast, keep in mind that you buck the norm. You challenge the proverbial status quo – it is what makes you – well, you. It is important that you recognize the very nature of bucking the status quo will have "repercussions" in terms of how you are perceived by others. They may need you to be a bit more open, so they can understand the deeper part of "you" better. The more open, understanding and patient you are with others, the easier it will be for them to accept and honor the uniqueness of you.

Failure

When your partner or spouse is a Failure, you must simply acknowledge their need to provide... even if it means they feel a need to work themselves into the ground. Admonishment that working so hard isn't necessary – while you deem such a statement shows your level of caring about the Failure – will have the exact opposite effect than you intend. Recognize that their career is directly tied to their worth.

At the same time, it's important to validate and acknowledge other "sides" – other successes outside of work – of the Failure to help them expand their own view of themselves beyond their careers. Maybe it's a compliment on handling a parenting challenge or interaction in a social setting that had nothing to do (including conversations) about his or her workplace or career. "You know, John, that little Johnny told me how much it meant to him for you to go along on the camping trip with the Scout troop. He said he really enjoyed being with you."

Showing admiration to a Failure scores points. Admiring their abilities, yes... even their work-aholic ones... is important to them. For the Unlikeable, it's about adoration, but for the Failure, it's simply admiration. Just let them know it.

If your HOS is Failure, understand that your value to your family is not just the dollars (or presents) you bring home. Often what the families of Failures crave most is quality time with you.

Bad

Those with the Bad HOS are the stringent rule followers. Understand that deviations from the rules are huge stressors for the Bads. However, like Unlovables' need to have their needs met and Incompetents' need to relax a little more, the Bads have a silent need to break away – even just a bit – from their strict code of always playing by the rules.

If you are in a relationship with a Bad, you will want to engage their silent need to be a little adventurous. It's silent and below the surface because they are always abiding by the rules and always doing the right thing. The Bads actually have a desire for at least a mild wild side. They look up to others who have wild side tendencies and can be a little careless – not over-the-top carelessness to the point at which a Bad will lose respect for the person – but someone who may become a little "untied" from time to time.

If you are someone with a Bad HOS, you will need to learn to allow a little bit of chaos and some rule bending in your life. If the house is messy, let it be that way while you go out and enjoy time with the family.

Consider the Pollyanna total-rule-follower type who falls for the "bad boy." They're exhibiting their admiration (albeit from afar) of the rule breaker and their wish that they had even the tiniest bit of similar tendencies. Perhaps, this is what is behind "opposites attract." However, their hijacker forces them to keep it all in check all the time and prove how good they are.

In your relationship with a Bad, try to draw this out a bit and help them embrace a little bit of "coloring outside the lines" because they do have a silent, if not secret, desire to do so.

However, you must also acknowledge that while this might occur (a bit of Bad rule breaking), the Bad needs law and order on a daily basis. Never take rule breaking or bending too far.

Ultimately, no matter what your HOS or that of your spouse or partner may be, relationship success is founded in honoring who you are with. The hardcore tendencies of each HOS type are likely what we find so appealing about them. Most couples that have been together for years recognize that the very traits that attract them to a partner can also become a source of contention.

No matter what the HOS type, it is important for both parties to acknowledge one another for the effort they put into the relationship (conscious or not). Acknowledgement is a form of acceptance of one another. The more we accept and acknowledge the most important person in our life, the more reward we get back.

Chapter Eighteen:
Your HOS in Business

First and foremost, business success is founded in relationships. Those relationships are probably not as deep or intimate as those that you have with your spouse or family; however, there are myriad relationships in business just the same, and as you read in the previous chapter, understanding your own Human Operating System as well as those of the people around you can either grease the skids or cause friction.

One source of equity in a business is the value in the relationships involved. Anyone in business knows and has experienced what a good relationship can do to a business and what damage a bad one can cause. The bad ones typically create a lot of distraction from our most valuable activities and also from cultivating great relationships with the good ones.

It is my belief that you are responsible for all of your outcomes, including the outcomes of the various relationships you have. If you find that your business is full of pain-in-the-neck clients and people – you are the source of it. If your business is filled with great people and great relationships – congratulations, you are also responsible for that.

Most entrepreneurs are running their businesses somewhat blindly. The crazy thing is that many successful business owners cannot tell you exactly what their success formula is in great detail. Because most people are unaware of their Human Operating Systems. Some of these successful folks have "gotten lucky" and have accidentally mastered using HOS types in business without understanding that they have done so. They intuitively know what works but are hard pressed to define or delineate why the things they are doing makes them successful.

I believe they are the exception, and that most of us go through every week, quarter, and year running our businesses blindly and struggling with the friction caused by HOS mismatches. Imagine how much more successful you would and could be if you understood how to leverage your own HOS type and those of your colleagues, peers, employees, and clients so there was a lot more "skid greasing" and much less friction.

As you have no doubt discerned having read this far, there are certain HOS types that fare very well in certain careers paths (and we've touched on those with the example stories I've shared), and conversely, there are HOS types that struggle in their careers *because* of their own Human Operating Systems. Whether you're the business owner or manager or the employee, most people chalk up a failed hire as a "bad fit" and don't think any more about it. You say "bad fit," but I contend that it's an HOS mismatch.

Consider all the bad hires that you've experienced throughout your career, and now imagine how understanding the ideal HOS that best fits the position could have helped avoid those missteps or at least provided you with the insight to counsel the employee to avoid their own self-sabotaging behaviors. Also, take a minute to think about all of the marketing dollars spent on failed marketing attempts or time wasted on unsuccessful networking events. I assure you, in both cases your HOS (or those of your target audiences) is at work, and fully understanding your HOS can help you more effectively navigate the various needs to build a successful business.

One Size Never Fits All

If you've ever purchased clothing touted as "one size fits all," you know it's either too big and baggy, too small and tight, or too long or too short. Occasionally, your size might fall in the sweet spot of the design and it fits just right, but that's rare and only left to chance. The same thing is true in business.

So many training programs available today offer this "one size fits all" approach to growing and managing your business. These programs often fail the businessperson, not because they fail to provide good content and ideas – they often do – but because they miss the most critical element to using any system, employing any concept, or enhancing any relationship: the impact of the Human Operating System. The very system running behind the scenes when using the ideas and skills that those training programs provide us.

Trying to plug a single marketing program into every business run by entrepreneurs with various HOS types is like trying to write one single piece of software that will work on every computer operating system. Let's take a minute to revisit where we started: a computer needs an operating system to run… not just to run effectively but to run at all. Humans are the same, and we're all running with various operating systems.

Consider the most simplistic analogy: the PC and the Mac. Each has a disparate OS (without even taking into consideration all of the various versions that have been developed over time). Yes, you can run the same programs on each – Microsoft Office, for example; however, the code behind that software has been specifically designed for the operating system on which it needs to run. Think about every software package you've ever purchased or every app you've ever downloaded. The very first thing you have to specify is the device and operating system on which you'll be using it. Of course, one size doesn't fit all!

Think of training programs, marketing initiatives and hiring decisions as what software or applications are to a computer. If we don't specify (or understand) which operating system it will be running on, how do you modify the program, idea or action steps effectively? Again, the reason I wrote this book came from the unique work my firm, Getting Results Coaching, does with each individual client. The very reason we don't run a cookie cutter program that we throw everyone into, is that it is not effective unless you recognize the value of individuality and personal design.

As I mentioned in the previous relationship chapter, there's a great deal of complexity, and the concepts, examples, and applications could indeed fill an entire book, but again, I would be remiss not to scratch the surface to help you at least begin to understand the impact that each HOS type has on business operations and in various business relationships.

Understanding how your HOS impacts each major area of your business, marketing, sales, hiring, and such, will certainly lead to greater success. Without this consideration, it is like loading new software on your computer or a new application on your phone without knowing if it will work effectively with their operating systems.

You'll recall that in sharing the stories of those people who I included in the chapters about each of the HOS types, we touched on their career choices. As with hiring decisions, some of their career choices were great matches for their particular HOS types and others, well, not so much.

Careers and Positions

Because of the demands, responsibilities, and tasks required in various careers, obviously some careers naturally and ideally lend themselves to various HOS types.

Leadership:

Of course, there is no surprise to the inclusion of the Powerless and Failures in leadership positions. The Powerless not only crave leadership, they thrive on it. Failures are very driven and winning matters. Both types are always in search of doing better and being better – better than others or than what they themselves were yesterday. Neither tends to be subservient.

Someone with a Weak HOS can also succeed in a leadership position; however, the Weak's abilities in the realm of client or customer service may be a mismatch, so the type of business the Weak leads is important, and the Weak will gain greater success when they leave customer service to someone else on the staff.

Because they set themselves up to be highly proficient in their respective areas, Incompetents can also succeed in leadership positions since that plays into their desire to be in control. That desire for control can provide a leadership stumbling block, however, with the Incompetents' possible inability to delegate and their "if I want it done right, I have to do it myself" thinking. Understanding this critical point will help an Incompetent work on a potential weakness, so they may thrive in a leadership role.

Client/Customer Service:

Unlikeables and Unlovables immediately come to mind to fill these rolls. Both HOS types thrive on making other people feel special and important, and what entrepreneur wouldn't want someone with that approach looking after clients? Unlikeables thrive on building contacts and Unlovables will do whatever it takes to meet the needs of others.

Incompetents and Bads also excel in these roles because of their extraordinary attention to detail. Both want everything to be letter-perfect, and you can always count on a Bad to follow every procedure without deviation.

It may surprise you to learn that Uglies also excel in this area. They are very detail-oriented people, and when it comes to good customer service and a great client experience, looking at and carrying out the fine details are what really drives success.

Sales:

Unlikeables certainly lead the way as sales people as they are very typically outgoing and gregarious. Unlikeables are also great at creating relationships and excel at "on the spot" sales or products and services that do not require a long sales cycle. However, Unlikeables may falter when it comes to follow up because they have concerns about "intruding" on the prospect, they hate to feel as though they are 'bothering' anyone; hence, greater success with "on the spot" sales. A successful match often occurs by pairing an Unlikeable as the sales person and one of the good customer service types (Incompetent, Bad, Ugly) as the account administrator.

On the other hand, a Failure in a sales role is driven to win, so they're not the type to take "no" for an answer. They can be persistent and they thrive on pursuing the sale.

Incompetents can also make good sales people, always casting their company and product, and by extension, themselves in the best possible light.

Research or Analyst

Dumbs are the best choice for positions that require specific and detailed knowledge. A financial analyst, medical researcher or other positions that require a detailed pursuit for answers is a good position for this HOS type.

I like to say, if you want the right answers and the research to back them up, hire a Dumb for the position. Just don't expect them to be the best choice for enhancing client relationships.

Marketing

When it comes to leveraging HOS types in the realm of marketing, we have to take into consideration both sides of it: the marketer and the audience – who's doing the talking and to whom we might be talking.

Back to the "one size fits all" thinking: In my line of work, there are a lot of training programs that espouse seminar marketing, especially in the financial industry. (You have no doubt, at one time, been sent a post care inviting you to a dinner to hear financial professionals speak on a relevant topic – this is a type of marketing.) You can have 100 advisors in the room listening to the same advice and processes regarding using seminars as a marketing vehicle. Invariably, part of the room takes the information and knocks it out of the park while the remainder looks back on it and deems it to have been a complete waste of their time and money and quite possibly a loss of a few years in which they could have been generating more revenue.

Knowing what I do about HOS types, I believe that those who are able to excel with this marketing are those in the Unlikeable and Unlovable arenas. The Powerless can also be successful here; however, they excel when endorsed by someone hosting the event. While the Powerless like to be in front of the room and in charge, they need to recognize that there is a great deal of detail required to make this type of marketing a success. A solid formula for this type of marketing (seminar marketing) would be a Powerless, Unlikeable or Incompetent at the head of the room speaking, an Ugly to set up the event (no detail forgotten), then an Unlovable, Incompetent or Bad to ensure the proper follow up.

Unlikeables can succeed with seminar marketing, but might lack in the follow up (they don't want to be a bother – people don't like that) which can undermine success.

In fact, I had an Unlikeable client who does seminars and enjoys them immensely. As a result, she had a very long list of – possibly 1,000 or more – prospects… but she had done nothing with them! I finally encouraged her to start following up with hand-written notes rather than starting with a phone call – an activity she avoided and dreaded because she was certain that was too obtrusive. The result? Prospects became clients, and her success really started to blossom. She was surprised when these prospects called her after receiving one of her "thoughtful, hand-written notes."

The key for yourself (or your employees) is to understand your HOS type and how that causes you to self-sabotage, then find ways around that behavior to create success… ala writing notes rather than calling.

If you choose to hold (or attend) networking events, again, consider the HOS types you're dealing with. When holding an event, like a mixer or wine and boutique event, look for an Ugly to coordinate and host it. With an Ugly at the helm, the event will indeed be memorable and every detail will shine.

When considering staff to attend general networking events, again, consider the HOS type. A Powerless may make an impression, but that person will likely come away with one or two new friends but few contacts and prospects to show for their effort. An Outcast is your better choice. They're looking to socialize and be with people. Unlikeables and Unlovables can also be very successful at these events with the same caveat noted regarding following up.

Cold-calling? Not many HOS types (or people in general) particularly enjoy this form of marketing. However, the HOS type that generally succeeds at this is the Failure. Their relentless, "don't give up" mentality allows them to power through the overwhelming number of objections that are encountered in this activity. They view it as a challenge to "win" by getting people to respond to them. Successful telemarketing is all about refusing to take "no" for an answer.

Now, think of the person on the other side of your marketing/sales efforts (the prospect). If you understand and can identify the HOS of others, it will help immensely with your efforts. What do the experts say? "Marketing is *ALL* psychology." Of course, you could have every HOS type represented in your marketing universe, and you can't easily tailor individual messages. However, think about your true target audience – your most ideal client. Think about who this person is, what drives them, and why they are a good fit for your business... and you've probably already done this for your marketing strategies.

There's a chance that your ideal client has a specific HOS. If so, I encourage you to revisit the various Human Operating Systems to determine what their fear is and develop your marketing message to address that. Again, this line of thinking and application of the HOS types could easily become its own book! For more information or guidance on this, visit www.TheHijacker.net to speak with someone who can help guide you more specifically around this vast topic.

Hiring

Understanding how Human Operating Systems work together or clash, for that matter, will help you hire more effectively.

As I said at the start of this chapter, there may be a handful of entrepreneurs who have hired successfully and created well-oiled and highly effective teams because they are making the best matches of HOS types without actually understanding that they've been doing so. Conversely, if you are struggling with clashes of what you might deem personality types in your own business, now is the time to use your new understanding of Human Operating Systems to reduce the friction.

For example, two Dumbs will find themselves consistently clashing over who has the most accurate facts, who is right, and who gets the accolades. On the other hand, having a Dumb on your team as a systems analyst, for example, can work quite well and truly pay off when knowledge and research are tremendous assets.

Similarly, imagine how much of a power struggle would occur if there were two Powerless HOS types in a partnership. In both examples, I guarantee there will be much time wasted because of the clash of Human Operating Systems that could otherwise be more constructively used for revenue-producing activities if there were a better HOS match between the parties involved.

We often hire people we like and, to be honest, that's a mistake. Since we generally tend to like people who are like us, the result is that we end up replicating personalities when, instead, we should be complementing them.

I have two clients who are partners in business, and one is an Unlikeable and the other an Unlovable. At first cut, you may think that they make a great team because they get along so well. The problem that I uncovered was, despite their extraordinary skill sets that should have created great success in financial services, they are only operating at about 15 to 20 percent of their effectiveness. Why? Because they are both very empathetic toward one another. When one has had a rough day, the other is quick to give them a pass to go home and "start over tomorrow." They are very permissive with each other, so every excuse is acceptable. That may work well for them at home, but certainly not in business.

However, get two Failures in a partnership together, and you'll have a completely different outcome. Granted, at the end of the day, dinner conversation may be non-existent if something occurred during the day that caused a clash, but in the long run, their business success will far exceed that of the Unlikeable/Unlovable partnership. A Powerless and an Unlikeable work well together as a team because the Powerless types like to delegate and the Unlikeables are happy to oblige.

If you hire an Incompetent, consider your own HOS first. While Incompetents are great with details and strive for perfection, they also like to hold the reins, and this can threaten anyone who has a need for full control.

Incompetents are not apt to relinquish that control easily, either.

When you're building out your team or when you have positions that you need to fill, think about the requirements of those positions and consider the strengths of each Human Operating System. If I need a rainmaker – someone to bring the relationship to me, I'm going to clearly lean toward an Unlikeable who loves to be out and about, chit chatting, and creating the contact. Follow up, as we've mentioned, is weaker, but if you bring the relationship to me, I can then hand it over to someone who excels at developing it further and closing the deal, like an Unlovable.

If I need a client service person to make sure all the details are handled, I'll look for an Incompetent or an Ugly. If I need a systems analyst, a Dumb will be high on my list of potential candidates because of their analytical abilities. They like to "show their numbers," create charts, and prove they're right.

With these examples, you can quickly see how using HOS types to build out your team, rather than hiring blindly, can move you toward success much faster… and with a lot less friction and headaches. Granted, there are other factors at play on any given resume and with any skill set; however, there is no doubt in my mind that considering someone's HOS is equally important for hiring and career-building success.

If you only hire people you tend to like, you're probably hiring people with the same HOS type, and while you may get along great every day, you probably won't see the results you want to achieve. If you feel you need further consultation on this contact me directly:

Lauren@TheHijacker.net

Chapter Nineteen:
Moving Forward from Here

My goal in writing this book was (and is) to help you live by design rather than default and to do things your way, in a more conscious way and to honor your own HOS rather than trying to combat it.

Self-sabotaging behaviors have likely plagued you up to this point by interfering with your goals and life dreams. When you operate in an unconscious mode, with your hijacker behind the wheel, you're simply living by default. You may have garnered success and have talent and a skill set that enables you to react effectively; however, you're still reacting, so you are not controlling the outcome. Reacting to the world and self-sabotaging are but two sides of the very same coin.

The danger is in believing you have effectively managed the hijacker but don't have a mentor, coach, or other professional who understands this concept and can recognize it before you do. Keep in mind your hijacker is the sneakiest sort! And remember the adage: you have never actually seen the back of your own head, only reflections of it in the mirror... and you need two mirrors to accomplish that goal. Two mirrors always provide a greater perspective and vantage point.

Up until now, you've possibly been asleep at the wheel. Your hijacker has been doing the driving, guiding you down the road of your life. It's time to apply what you've learned about your own HOS type to unseat him and take control.

I believe the book you've just finished truly represents the diagnostic code that you need to finally stop self-sabotaging and get out of your own way. When you understand your own Human Operating System, you've opened the door to unseat your hijacker and truly break the patterns and take control of your life.

Of course, it won't happen overnight, and it won't happen without effort. I assure you that the results are worth it. When you begin to apply what you've learned about managing your mind, you will have created the path you need to move toward the life of your own design and choosing. With mind management comes the ability to unseat that hijacker, wrest control, and get what you want out of life.

When you more fully understand (and accept) your Human Operating System, you gain the ability to remove those small targets that continually pop up in front of your line of sight and stay focused on the bigger targets that ultimately create a vivacious life that is extremely rewarding. By managing your HOS, you can begin to stop yourself from the actions and behaviors that have either led you in the wrong direction or stopped you in your tracks. As I've said, nobody sets out on any given day to sabotage their own efforts and ruin the chance of getting what they want. Whether what you want is a lifelong fulfilling relationship or balancing great success with the ability to enjoy it without the constant fear of losing it all, putting the hijacker in his place is the key to it all. You can count on the fact that your hijacker will attempt to fight your efforts unless you remain mindful of its tendencies. Your hijacker is continually going to try to redirect your focus to the small targets (the 8x10 sheet of paper) because your hijacker is a survivalist, and if he can keep you focused on the small, self-sabotaging targets, he wins. He maintains control... and you end up living by default. However, when you master managing your HOS, *YOU* win by being able to live a highly fulfilling life.

A recent client of mine said it well. At just 22 years old, she said, "I feel like this is what a real breakthrough means. I can now see how my mind goes back and forth like a conversation. That conversation used to take me down a path of constant stress, worry and concern. Now that I can manage that dialogue in my brain, I see things more clearly. I now know what direction to take and am confident because I see how it fits into my bigger picture (think big target). I also recognize others around me who are like sleepwalking zombies, reacting to whatever life throws at them – they are puppets to their emotions and inadvertently created messes in their lives by reacting to those negative emotions. You really are able to create your own world, one that works *for* you when you learn to manage your hijacker."

It thrills and excites me to see such young people "getting it." Just as they are choosing their careers, their lifelong mates and the experiences along the way, they can do so better armed with greater consciousness and clarity.

You too can start to embrace and leverage all the positive attributes that come with your HOS. You can't get through life without one, you can't trade it in for a different one... and when you truly understand your HOS, you won't want to! Your HOS brings with it great abilities, so it's certainly to your benefit to more clearly understand what they are and how you can use them to your advantage.

The power of understanding and managing your HOS is so great, that when you apply what you have learned in this book – you will finally have the opportunity to lead a highly fulfilling life. The opportunity here is not to create a short-term fix where you "feel good" for a while but to live out the rest of your days in a way that allows you to suck the sweet nectar out of life – leaving you with the most vibrant experience life has to offer.

Share this book with everyone you know – because as they become aware of their own HOS and how it relates to their world around them, your world just gets better. Living in a world of unconscious zombies who flip you off in traffic when you didn't hit the gas fast enough at a green light or who argue with you over seemingly simple or even stupid subjects can be challenging. You may constantly feel like, "Why don't they get it? Why can't they see how ridiculous they are being?" Once those around you with whom you interact most on a daily basis – co-workers, spouses, friends and family members – recognize and manage their own hijackers, your world improves right along with theirs. It's not easy to live in a world full of zombies, but it is very rewarding to live with highly conscious people aware of their hijackers' tendencies and who have the ability to manage them.

I encourage you to re-read any chapters you may need to in order to fully digest and incorporate this concept and its impact on your life. Talk about the things you begin to notice around you with friends or family members who have also read the book. The concept of a Human Operating System or the mental hijacker is novel and one you've probably never considered previously. It can be complicated, just as the code that goes into a computer operating system is complicated.

Word of Caution: Your mind along with its operating system is present when reading this book. Your hijacker may attempt to interfere with internalizing the message or it may just be too big a challenge to figure out what your HOS is or how to manage it. I don't want to leave you high and dry. Again, my commitment in writing this book was to provide you with whatever tools necessary to help you create a life by design. Should you need additional support processing your HOS, please visit: www.TheHijacker.net

After working with hundreds of clients over the years, I have seen this process effectively transform lives and businesses. My clients are living proof of what kind of life managing your HOS can turn out. They have been my inspiration for writing this book. It is my way of paying it forward and helping as many people as possible live a more conscious and rewarding life.

Resources:

Meditation Podcasts:

The Meditation Station:
https://itunes.apple.com/us/podcast/my-meditation-station/id123885923?mt=2

Qigong Meditation
https://itunes.apple.com/us/podcast/qigong-meditation-podcast/id119788564?mt=2

Meditation Oasis
https://www.meditationoasis.com/podcast/

Coaching/Consultation

www.TheHijacker.net
www.GettingResultsInc.com

95962232R00124

Made in the USA
Columbia, SC
27 May 2018